# TALES OF A BROADWAY FLACK

★ ★ ★

## THE CHARMED LIFE OF PRESS AGENT
## SOL JACOBSON

# BY DAVID A. LONG

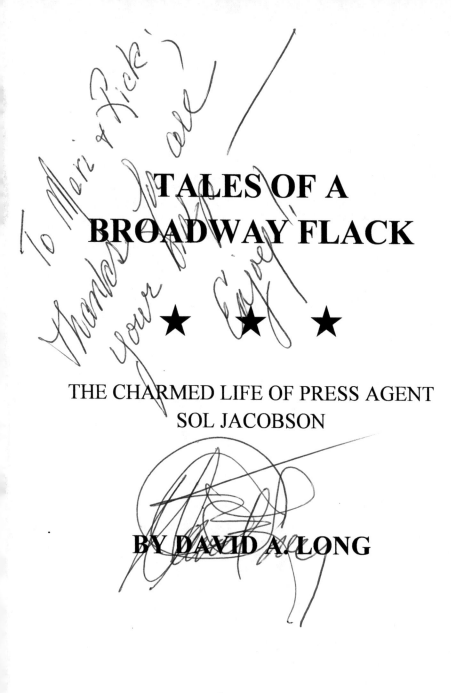

∞ INFINITY
PUBLISHING

Copyright © 2011 by David A. Long

ISBN 0-7414-6810-7

Printed in the United States of America

Published October 2011

∽

INFINITY PUBLISHING
1094 New DeHaven Street, Suite 100
West Conshohocken, PA 19428-2713
Toll-free (877) BUY BOOK
Local Phone (610) 941-9999
Fax (610) 941-9959
Info@buybooksontheweb.com
www.buybooksontheweb.com

**Dedicated to:**


My wife of 56 years, Patty Ann Long,
my true love and PAL, and the world's
greatest editor

and

To my wonderful four sons, their wives
and 12 amazing grandchildren
who keep me young

# Introduction

Sol Jacobson was, in the vernacular of the book you're about to read, a flack—an affectionate description of a breed of theatre press agent who is part of the rich, ancient history of a theatre community that's gone, but not forgotten. There were producers in those days who managed to present a play or musical every single season and each attraction was easily identified as "Kermit Bloomgarden's" or "The Theatre Guild's" or "Feuer and Martin's" or "David Merrick's. They put their money in support of their taste.

I began my association with Sol when George Abbott, Jerome Weidman, Jerry Bock, and Sheldon Harnick were writing FIORELLO!, a musical celebrating New York's flamboyant and extraordinarily accomplished mayor. I produced it with my partner Bobby Griffith and it opened on Broadway on November 23, 1959 and it remains one of the few musicals to win the Pulitzer Prize. Sol went on to represent all my musicals up to and including FIDDLER ON THE ROOF which opened on September 22, 1964 and closed 3,242 performances later. It broke all records at that time.

Playwrights were equally prolific in those days and were almost guaranteed that whatever they wrote would show up on stage the following season. Producers had their favorite actors and directors and even designers were connected to the artistic vision of a producer. Frequently, I had three shows running simultaneously on Broadway and Mr. Merrick had more than six. All this activity required me to have a staff casting director and, from 1958 through 1973, my staff press agent was Sol Jacobson.

*The New York Times'*; ABC ads were uncompetitive, alphabetical listings of plays and musicals and very rarely did anyone ever purchase more than a quarter or half-page quote ad on Sunday. The *Times'*; reporter, a man named Sam Zolotow, appeared in your office always unannounced. He rooted about, looking for items of interest: new productions planned, cast replacements, directorial assignments, and, of course, theatre bookings. He was as tough and cynical as the fellas in THE FRONT PAGE, able to discount your denials and report what he thought on good authority. Still, I miss him. As I miss Sol Jacobson. And everything else in the theatre of the '30s and '40s which I worshipped as a schoolboy until I became a producer in the '50s and a director in the '60s.

I assumed, given all the activity in my office, Sol would stay on forever. But he chose to leave after FIDDLER because he did not want to be exclusive to any one producing/directing office and I respected that.

These memoirs are a rich account of that period when Broadway was a community—when we weren't so damned competitive because there was room for all of us. Times have changed and that will only be evident after you've read this warm, compelling history of THEN.

In reading this book, I'm reminded of an anecdote some years later when I directed Arthur Kopit's END OF THE WORLD, an excellent, somewhat unappreciated play. Near the end of rehearsals, I found myself apologizing to the cast for mentioning "the good old days" too frequently. But then, the youngest actress in the company raised her hand and said: "Don't apologize, Hal. Every one of us knows that it <u>was</u> better then." And it was.

Hal Prince
June 7, 2011

# Author's Prerogative:

I think there is nothing worse than wanting to get into a book and having to read multiple pages of explanatory notes. With this in mind, I promise the reader: this will only be one page.

Sol Jacobson and I lived at Foulkeways in Gwynedd at the same time. For years Sol regaled me with his wonderful stories of Broadway and his part as press agent, known in the trade as a flack. I suggested that he let me put his delightful stories down on paper so that his children and others would have the pleasure of knowing them. Time was of the essence for neither of us was getting any younger; he, 96 and I, 78. He agreed and we began our trip down memory lane in 2009.

Because Sol was such a great raconteur I felt the book should be written in his voice. That is why I chose to write his memoirs in the first person.

I do hope you enjoy reading this book as much as I did writing it. Sol Jacobson was a real *mensch* in the full sense of the word.

**David A Long**

## Prologue

### "Hey kid, loan me 50 cents"

*"Hey kid, loan me 50 cents?"*

*This is what Milton Berle said to me as we walked down Sixth Avenue, having cut over from 47th Street and the Biltmore Theater.*

*I forked over two quarters and he ducked into a cigar store on the corner and emerged puffing on a cigar.*

*"I'll pay you later," he said airily.*

*Milton was playing the lead part of Arthur Lee in a George Abbott comedy, See My Lawyer. Ezra Hunt, another budding radio star, had staged it. In the cast were Teddy Hart, an Abbott regular, and Gary Merrill.*

The year was 1939 and Broadway was looking up. We were coming out of the Great Depression and things actually seemed rosy.

As an ambitious associate press agent in George Abbott's office, working for the veteran Phyllis Perlman, I had booked Berle for an interview on something new. They called it Television. The studio was an upstairs room over a cigar store in a two-story building on the west side of Sixth Avenue between 42nd and 43rd Streets. There was no elevator, just a dingy set of stairs; not even a balustrade.

These were the early days of television when RCA, Philco and GE were manufacturing the massive wooden cabinets that held the multitude of tubes that transformed the TV signal into the small picture tube displayed at the top of the set. The TV industry was trying its best to attract viewers.

The location of the sending station was in Palisades, NJ and the few who had TV sets in New York City reported they could watch their small TV picture on the West side of town if no big buildings were in the way.

The interview went well and I had primed Milton to be sure he mentioned the title of our production and where it was playing. I watched on a monitor through a haze of cigar smoke, listening to Berle's continual patter. Fortunately, he did come through with the essentials.

When he finished the stint we parted; he headed up to the Friars Club and his buddies and I returned to the RCA Building and the calm of the Abbott office.

Little did I dream that within a decade, the NBC Building next door would be home to NBC-TV Studios and that the same, brash Mr. Berle would become its first super star, playing in his own slot, "The Milton Berle Show."

I'm still waiting for that 50 cents that Milton owes me and I just wonder what it would be worth today if I had put it in my daughter Judy's bank account, instead of giving it to Milton.

# ★ Contents: ★

## ACT I

### My beginnings, youth, young adulthood and entrance into the world of Broadway Theater ........... 1

Scene *1*: From whence I came .............. 3

Scene *2*: I became a man .................. 11

Scene *3*: Jasper Deeter; the Hedgerow Theater .............. 17

Scene *4*: Cupid Strikes .......... 25

Scene *5*: Married at 23 .......... 31

Scene *6*: The Hedgerow Bus and Truck Tour .............. 37

Scene *7*: My first paying jobs ............ 43

Scene *8*: Summer in New Hampshire .............. 53

## ACT II

### My Early Career on Broadway .............. 57

Scene *1*: My first job in New York, New York .............. 59

Scene *2*: C.P. Greneker and the Shuberts .............. 67

Scene *3*: Bucks County Playhouse .......... 83

Scene *4*: My Nine months with George Abbott .............. 97

Scene *5*: Arsenic .............. 103

Scene *6*: The King of Press Agents, Richard Sylvester Maney ........ 111

Scene *7*: "Salutes" .............. 123

Scene *8*: Maurice Evans, English Import .............. 129

Scene *9*: Female Flacks .............. 139

Scene *10*: Tennessee Williams .............. 147

Scene *11*: Joseph Aloysius Flynn .............. 155

Scene *12*: Drafted at age 32 .............. 167

# ACT III

## *Broadway and My Golden Years* ..................... *187*

*Scene 1*: *Jacobson, Doll and Harmon* .............................. *189*

*Scene 2*: *Judy's Birthday party and The National Theater of Greece* ............. *203*

*Scene 3*: *Our Greenwich Village Brownstone* ................... *211*

*Scene 4*: *Look Back in Anger and the Entertainer* ............ *217*

*Scene 5*: *West Side Story* ................................................ *227*

*Scene 6*: *Fiorello, Take Her, She's Mine and A Funny Thing Happened on the Way to the Forum* ...................... *237*

*Scene 7*: *Dawson City and Foxy* ...................................... *247*

*Scene 8*: *A Silver Lining* ................................................ *259*

*Scene 9*: *Fiddler on the Roof* .......................................... *267*

# ACT IV

## *Enjoying Retirement* ................................ *283*

*Scene 1*: *Long Lake, New York* ........................................ *285*

*Scene 2*: *Foulkeways, my home: A Continuing Care Retirement Community (CCRC)* ............................. *303*

*Scene 3*: *Key West, Florida* ............................................. *323*

*Scene 4*: *Words of Love and Life* ..................................... *333*

# *ACT I*

★ ★ ★

## *My beginnings, youth, young adulthood and entrance into the world of Broadway Theater*

*Fanny Jacobson with Baby*
*Solomon A. Jacobson*

*From whence I came*

I was born on July 3$^{rd}$, 1912; I was no fire-cracker, for my mother was English and had no idea that she should hold out until the 4$^{th}$ so I could be an "Independence Baby."

My parents were in their forties when they married and I was their only issue. The combination of older parents and a single child resulted in "the spoiled child syndrome."

My father, who was born in Mechanicsburg, PA, was a successful clothier on Market Square in downtown Harrisburg.

Solomon Jacobson, his father, had a more colorful background. He came to the United States from Germany but, before settling in Mechanicsburg, PA as a young man, he first went West to seek his fortune in California during the Gold Rush of 1849. To get there he rode a mule-train across the Isthmus of Panama to the Pacific and was fortunate not to pick up malaria on the way as did so many others. Then onto a sailing ship that took him up the coast into Sacramento Bay. A tailor by trade, he decided against being a miner but instead made pants, shirts and suits for the gold seekers like one of his fellow countrymen, Levi Strauss. But unlike Levi Strauss, who coined the name blue jeans and Levis to be synonymous with working denim pants, and built an industry, my grandfather remained a tailor and resettled after the Gold Rush Era in Mechanicsburg, PA. The family legend insists he learned all his English by reading Shakespeare as he plied his trade, placing the open book across his knees, a practice that he kept up for the rest of his life.

The Kuhn Store was established in Harrisburg in the early 1900s. Sam Kuhn needed a tailor to alter the clothes he sold and he turned to his old friend, Solomon Jacobson, the tailor who read Shakespeare while he tailored, to shorten pants, take a coat in here and there or what have you. The goods were delivered by messenger to Solomon's tailor shop but, when returned to the Kuhn Store, young Morris, Solomon's son, was pressed into service. Sam Kuhn took a liking to young Morris and in time Morris became an employee of the Kuhn Store. After Sam Kuhn's death, Morris and Sam's nephew, Albert Kirsheler, took over the store.

For many years we lived in a double house on the north side of Harrisburg; 2129 North 2$^{nd}$ Street, to be exact. The house had been built as a twin with separate families living on each side. My Father turned it into a single dwelling which allowed him

4

to build a comfortable library on the second floor. It was here he would take refuge, dressed in his smoking jacket, sitting in his Morris chair smoking his pipe, with his feet up on the ottoman.

The house size allowed room for our maid, and I can't remember any time during my childhood when we were without a full time servant who cooked and cleaned.

The house no longer stands, washed out by one of the many floods from the Susquehanna River; or it well might have exploded! Yes, that's what happened in those days. Home owners, seeing the rising waters invade their homes, would abandon them, forgetting to turn off their cellar furnaces. The mixture of flooding waters and the furnace gases was all that was needed for a big boom and no more houses.

When I was a young boy, Father would send Mother and me to the Breakers Hotel in Atlantic City, NJ, for the summer. Those were the days of the luxurious Atlantic City Hotels such as The Ambassador, The Brighton, The Chelsea and The Shelburne, to name just a few. This is where the well-to-do would spend their summers, enjoying the ocean breezes and the salt air and spending time either walking or riding in the ubiquitous rattan carts or "rolling chairs," pushed by men looking for summer employment.

I hated being there. There was little for a lone youngster to do and the "old ladies," my Mother's friends, would spend their time playing bridge or mahjong or just relaxing in rocking chairs on the porch overlooking the Boardwalk, watching the constant stream of vacationers as they ambled by. When they did, I would sneak out and head for the beach to watch the airplanes. But my favorite pastime was to find some theater that was in rehearsal. Then up through the open fire escape I would go, and into the theater to sit and watch. One of my favorite stars was Eddie Cantor. What a showman! I guess it was here that I was bitten by the dreaded "drama bug" from which I never did recover.

When I was older, Father and Mother felt a camp experience at Camp Idlewild, on Schroon Lake in the Adirondack Mountains of NY, would be good for me. I thought anything would be better than having to endure another summer in Atlantic City with the "old ladies" even though I did enjoy the salt water taffy.

I enjoyed camp, spending most of my time in the drama section. I even had the opportunity to organize a show and play a number of roles.

Getting to camp was an experience with a capital "E." From Harrisburg to the Adirondacks by plane or car is no trip at all, these days. But in 1924, neither means of transportation was available. Cars were just coming into their own and planes, well, what sane person would board one of those?

We, and I say we, because it was I and Richard Goldsmith, (the child of friends of my parents) who traveled together. Richard, who was three-and-a half-years my junior, was placed in my charge "so that he wouldn't get lost," according to the Sr. Goldsmiths.

We boarded the train in Harrisburg, traveling through Newark, NJ, to our destination, Hoboken. Then onto busses for a quick trip to the Jersey Meadows Station where we met the night boat to Albany. Richard and I berthed together for the night but sleep was out of the question; pillow fights, and just having fun and raising hell was much more interesting than a good night's sleep. From Albany, NY, the Delaware and Hudson Railroad, or the Dirty and Hot as we called it, transported us into the Adirondacks, dumping us and all our camp trunks at Essex Junction, NY. Finally, after twenty-four hours, we arrived at Schroon Lake and Camp Idlewild.

*I'm the tall camper in the middle*

While I was growing up, Harrisburg was a bustling and viable city, one of the most industrialized cities in the Northeast. Harrisburg, capital of

Pennsylvania, was the junction of trains going north, south, east and west with the largest employer being the railroad system, followed by the iron and steel industries.

During the early part of the 20th century, and thanks to the efforts of some of Harrisburg's leading citizens, a movement to beautify the city began, resulting in the creation of Riverfront Park, Reservoir Park, the Italian Lake and Wildwood Park plus the beautification of the expanded Capital complex.

So prominent had the city become that, during WWI, the Navy honored the city by naming one of its ships the USS Harrisburg.

Although the horse and buggy was the common means of transportation, two elderly ladies down the street did own an electric car. Henry Ford's gas Model T, know as the "Tin Lizzy was in production to be followed in 1927 by the Model "A". Both cars were, for the first time, mass produced on an assembly line.

My bachelor Uncle, David, had the only automobile in our family and it was a Willys-Knight, a luxury automobile manufactured in Cleveland. He lived in Mechanicsburg, owned and operated a country store and was a watchmaker by trade. On Sundays, with regularity, he would take us for drives in the country.

I was very fond of Uncle David, and always felt I was lucky enough to have two fathers. Spoiled or not, I look back on my childhood as a happy one.

Judy and Babs, my cute little girls, ages 12 and 6, looked at my Uncle Dave quite differently. From their perspective, he was a typical old bachelor who didn't care very much for the younger generation. They reported he never cracked a smile and when they saw him coming they would say, "Here comes sour puss." Babs remembers that he was always fixing clocks. If she dared to knock on his workshop door while he was working, he would comment; "Go away." Regarding his pride and joy, his automobile, the girls were allowed to stand on the running board if they didn't touch anything.

Uncle David spent a lifetime collecting pistols but never fired a weapon in his life. His collection depicted the history of the pistol dating back to the Civil War. He spent years traveling around the state buying up old pistols from farmers and merchants. He even had a copy of the pistol that killed President Lincoln. Polished and mounted on wood, his display took over an entire wall of his home and it was one of his most prized possessions.

Did you ever do something that you lived to regret? Well, I did by not accepting his collection when he offered it to me. It was right after WWII, and I had been assigned to an infantry regiment. The very thought of anything to do with shooting or killing was anathema to me, so I turned him down cold with a "No way."

*Scene* **2**

*I became a man*

At age 13 I was called to the Torah. My Bar Mitzvah was held at Temple Ohev Shalom, the German Jewish Reform Temple in Harrisburg, where our family belonged and where my father had been president. According to Jewish custom, I, in becoming a Bar Mitzvah, the "Son of the Commandment," was considered to be taking on a man's responsibilities and obligations.

The following year I worked hard, becoming an Eagle Scout. One of the 21 merit badges was "Journalism." To fulfill that requirement I worked at our local paper, *The Courier*, editing AP copy from the teletype. I obtained the job thanks to my Uncle David's friends and owners, the Lowengards. The paper was printed once a week, on Sunday. Looking back, at the age of 14, I was extremely naïve and now I wonder what services I could have rendered.

But I did fulfill my requirement and became an Eagle Scout.

One of the stories I worked was of two gay men who lived in a railroad caboose. One had been murdered. I ended up "murdering" the story, for I had no idea what "gay" meant. My understanding of the word gay was "light-hearted or "happy."

While I was working on my Eagle Scout badge for journalism, I was selected to attend a Boy Scout weekend conference in New York, sponsored by the Columbia School of Journalism. It was quite an honor, for Columbia was considered to be one of the best journalism schools in the East at the time. The commitment required that I, as one of the participants, write a story about my experience in New York and wire it back to Gus Steinmetz, editor of the Harrisburg *Telegraph*, so he could print it in the local paper.

I filled the commitment but with one caveat; I wrote my Saturday article in advance and wired it back to Harrisburg, which left me my Saturday afternoon free. If I cut the afternoon conference class, which I found rather boring, I could do what I wanted to do, like seeing a Broadway show.

Gray's Drug Store at 42nd Street near 7$^{th}$ Avenue was an easy walk from the "Y" at 34$^{th}$ Street where I was staying. I knew that I could obtain a cut-rate ticket at Joe Leblang's "Central and Public Service Theater Ticket Office" located in the basement of Gray's. It was the practice of New York theaters to allow Leblang to "dump" tickets at a cheap price in order to fill their theaters.

A single ticket to *A Connecticut Yankee* was available, and I took it. What a treat. It was my first Rodgers and Hart musical. The book was by Herbert Fields who adapted the show from *A Connecticut Yankee in King Arthur's Court* by Mark Twain. To this day I still can sing some of the hit songs, "Thou Swell," "On a Desert Island with Thee" and "I Feel at Home with You."

My parents enjoyed going abroad in the summer to visit my mother's relatives, the Goldmans, and then travel to the Continent. The trip was always made on a Cunard Liner because my Mother wanted to support the British.

When my parents left for the Continent, I stayed behind in England with my cousin Arthur, the youngest of the Goldmans' three boys, in Golders Green, near Hampstead Heath, in the northwest section of London.

Arthur and I were amused by the sight of a "little fat guy" who, every morning, would walk by our house on the way to work. We never dared to stop him to chat, for his walk was brisk and he was quite focused on where he was going. I learned from my aunt that he was a neighbor and none other than that great movie–maker, Alfred Hitchcock, hurrying to the Hallstead Silent Film Company.

My cousin and I went often to the silent movies where the dialogue was in printed captions on the screen. Sound was not introduced until 1927. Can you imagine sitting in a movie theater and listening to a film for the first time? That was a revolutionary innovation. And the silent movie actors were befuddled by this new sound track. The movie industry had to find stage actors to fill the roles for their sound movies because they were better at acting and could remember the lines better than the "Charlie Chaplins" of the day. Some of the actors were like Rudolph Valentino who couldn't even speak English, or like Ramón Novarro, who had a flagrantly affected gay lisp.

In the late summer, the Goldmans moved to their summer home in West End, a riverside resort in Essex County where the regimental or military band entertained us every night in the local band stand.

Arthur showed great interest in music, studied the violin and later became first violinist for the Birmingham Symphony Orchestra. Tragically, he died during the war. Arthur had converted to Quakerism and became a conscientious objector. He was sent to a fruit farm in southern England where he became a farm hand. He died during his employment and they traced his death to the effects of the chemical spray used on the fruit.

In the summer of 1929, our family, before heading off to England, made a stop in New York City. We spent a few days there taking in the sights and sounds of the Big City before embarking. As a special treat, my father suggested we see a movie, because the New York movie theaters used a full orchestra in the pit while showing their silent films rather than the single usual piano player.

"No," I suggested to my Father, "let's see a live show." *Show Boat* had opened the previous

December and I was familiar with all the songs because I had played my Victor records of the show so many times on my windup Victrola.

The Victrola was to the kids of my day what the "I Pod" is to the youth of today and I spent hours listening to my collection of 78 rpm records.

The Victrola consisted of a turntable which held the record and a tone-arm which picked up the sound off the record and amplified the sound through a speaker. To make the turntable go, the operator used a crank to wind-up a spring which propelled the turntable. The records, made of a petroleum based product were brittle and could easily crack. Because they were so fragile, they were placed on the turntable very carefully. The tone-arm was extended over the record and, at the same time, the head, or soundbox, was flipped into position so that the steel needle engaged the first groove. With practice, this would happen without a hitch. If not, the needle might not seat and would fly across the record, making its own groove. The next time the record was played it would stick in one place playing the section over and over again, making a terrible noise of plop, plop, plop until it was physically moved to the next groove. And the needles; they had to be changed regularly, which meant loosening the thumbscrew, removing the old needle and replacing it. Invariably, the needle, which was sharp and small, would puncture your finger, and I had the wounds to prove it.

Primitive, yes, by our standards today. But for our generation, the Victrola was a constant source of enjoyment.

The performance of *Show Boat* we saw was spectacular, with Jules Bledsoe playing the part of Joe, singing "Ol' Man River." Paul Robeson, for whom the song was written and who made the song famous at a later date, was unavailable due to other commitments.

I was hooked; even at age 17 I knew my place would be in the theater. It was my destiny!

*Jasper Deeter; the Hedgerow Theater*

It was the Dartmouth Alumni Association that recruited me to attend its alma mater. Colleges were hard pressed to fill their schools during The Depression, and it was the alumni's job to round up students who could afford to go. I started at Dartmouth, in Hanover, NH, in the Fall of 1930 and became involved in the Dartmouth Players and was also a reporter for *The Dartmouth*, the oldest college newspaper in the country, founded in 1799.

In my freshman year I remember a slightly built, balding boot salesman, who came through the dormitory halls of Dartmouth shouting, "Ski boots, 10 dollars, Ski boots, 10 dollars." He traveled with a roll of paper under his arm and, if you wished to purchase his boots, the paper quickly descended to the floor. It was on this paper, with you in your stocking feet, that the "Boot-man" deftly drew an outline of your foot, labeled it and, within a week, you received a pair of boots that were guaranteed for life; all for ten bucks.

In those days, the boot salesman traveled from one college to another selling his wares. He was based in Freeport, ME where he and his brother ran a small clothing store. His name was Leon L. Bean. Mr. Bean went on to become one of the largest merchandisers in the country, known as the LL Bean Co.. By the end of the last century its gross billing had reached $ 1 billion. The company put Freeport on the map and made it into the popular outlet town it is today.

During Christmas vacation of my first year I was looking for a summer job in acting. So, my father, who knew Ted Deeter, a Mechanicsburg plumbing supply dealer, arranged a date with Ted's brother, Jasper Deeter, the founder/director of the internationally known Hedgerow Theater in Rose Valley, PA. Both boys had grown up in Mechanics-burg, PA. At the time, Jasper was directing Penn's "The Mask and Wig Show" at the Wilmington Playhouse, trying it out before its opening in Philadelphia. He said he'd see me between acts if I came back stage. I did and he hired me on the spot, saying, "I'll take anyone named Solomon Jacobson." "Why is that, Mr. Deeter?" I asked. "Your grandfather was the only man in Mechanicsburg, PA, who read Shakespeare as he sat in his tailor shop window, sewing with the book propped on his knees," he answered.

And that's how my serious actor/publicist career began. I learned a great deal that summer of '31, performing character actor roles. Little did I know at that time how integrated into the Hedgerow scene I would become and that I would be with the organization for five years. I also learned more about Jasper Deeter, the person, and gained a great respect for this remarkable, theatrical innovator.

Jasper Deeter was indeed born in Mechanicsburg, PA, in 1893, the grandson of a successful auto parts magnate. The Deeter family was filled with achievers; his brother Ted built a plumbing supply company, his sister Ruth became an MD and became medical director of a TB Sanatorium, and his sister Jane would, in 1919, become the National Director of the Girl Scouts of America.

Jasper, on the other hand, was floundering during his late teens and early twenties, not knowing what he would do. It wasn't until his middle 20's that he found his true calling, that of acting. He had been expelled from Dickinson College and had failed in a career as a reporter. Seeing actor James O'Neill in the production of *The Count of Monte Cristo* turned the tide for him. It convinced Jasper that he wanted to act and he soon became successful, moving into leading roles such as that of Ned

Melloy in the play *The Exorcism,* written by Don Taylor.

Jasper also met Eugene ONeill, James O'Neill's son, who at the time was a fledgling playwright. Eugene, who had recently been kicked out of Princeton, was boarding with Jasper's sister, Jane Deeter Rippen, while James and his wife were touring the country playing in *The Count of Monte Cristo.* The two young men became devoted friends and Jasper was given the supporting role of Henry Smithers in the original production of O'Neill's *Emperor Jones,* which premiered in the Province-town Playhouse in Greenwich Village on November 20, 1920. The play was highly successful, ran for 204 performances and launched Eugene O'Neill's career as a famous playwright.

History was made that day; Jasper and Eugene were among those who decided that a black actor should be used in the title role of Brutus Jones, the Emperor, rather than a white actor in blackface. That was not the custom of the day and the result was a breakthrough for black actors in the American theater.

In 1924 Jasper parted company with his friend. Eugene insisted that they move the play uptown rather than keeping it at the Playhouse Theater. Jasper was just as adamant that they keep the play in Greenwich Village.

At age 31, Jasper moved to Philadelphia, just south of Rose Valley, to pursue his idea, that of a repertory theater. He also wished to be closer to his other sister, Ruth who, as a physician, had founded and now managed one of the first tuberculosis sanitariums in the country. One day while riding through the countryside with his sister, she suggested that he look at The Hutton Mill, which had been abandoned. He did and his dream came to fruition; the Hedgerow Theater was born and became the most famous and the longest-lived regional repertory theater in the United States. It attracted all kinds of theatrical people; playwrights, actors, set designers, electrical designers. All wanted to study and learn from Jasper Deeter.

Deeter brought several actors with him from Provincetown one of whom, Ann Harding, became a film star in the early "talkies." It was she who named the theater when she said, "If they won't let us play in the theater, we can always act under the hedgerows."

Until I walked down Rose Valley Road on that June day in 1931, I had never before seen the magical place called the Hedgerow Theater. When I arrived, the theater doors were open but nobody was around except a burly guy hauling set flats up through the trapdoor. I soon found out that his name was Harry Bellaver and I was startled to learn he would play the title role that night in Eugene O'Neills' *The Hairy Ape.* His punched-in-face made him ideal for the ocean liner stoker. He had been kicked by a mine mule in his native Illinois. For the rest of his life he would be cast as the tough guy. Bellaver would become a prolific film character actor beginning in 1939 and lasting through the 1960s. Some of his more notable roles were in *From Here to Eternity, The House on Ninety-Second Street* and *Side Street.* He is also remembered for his part as Sitting Bull in Irving Berlin's *Annie Get Your Gun,* starring Ethel Merman, where his sole line was, "No put money in show biz."

I learned my first day that actors at the Hedgerow are jacks-of-all-trades and do it all; acting, moving scenery or whatever needs doing. My first night on the job, I washed dishes after dinner. That was a new experience for me; my parents always had a maid and that was her duty, not mine.

I soon learned that living conditions at Hedgerow were like those of a summer camp. We even found ourselves, if there were not enough beds for the actors, taking a trip by car ten miles south and sleeping at Deeter's sister's sanitarium, which we nicknamed the "San." I wonder now, knowing how contagious TB can be, if anyone ever thought about the consequences of placing young adults in such an environment?

As for compensation for work rendered; there was no pay check. However, a minimal stipend was given to anyone who worked. But that really didn't matter; if we were allowed to work in Deeter's theater, directed by the master, that's all we wanted. We were mesmerized by our leader, driven to the stage by the Deeter philosophy. We enjoyed working for this dreamer who had striking good looks, deep-set brown eyes and a voice like a small-town preacher of the Gospel.

Our stage had been designed by Deeter many years before my arrival, but its uniqueness needs mentioning. The Deeter stage came apart to allow different levels down to the auditorium floor. Beside the proscenium, the main part of the stage, were additional entrances which members of the company called "Shakespeares" because, when they opened up, the playing area looked like the old Globe Theater. Curving around the upper stage was a plaster dome, copied from the one at the Province-town Theater. Although it restricted the backstage work area, the dome had light projectors that could create changing scenic effects. Actors heard a flattering new resonance in their own voices as they worked in front of this dome. There being no "fly" space above the stage, sets were raised from the cellar through a large hatch in the stage floor, on a hand-operated winch elevator. Deeter's good friend Wharton Esherick, an artisan who would become famous for his creative work in wood, built the continuous spiral stairwell that led the actors and technicians to the backstage level and on up to the lightbridge.

Always in Deeter's mind was the idea of repertory. Theater was changing. The great theater companies of Moscow and Dublin had come to New York and brought with them new insights into the art of ensemble acting. What Deeter needed were actors who would live and work together in communal obscurity for little or no pay for the chance to perfect their craft; to hoe potatoes one day and play King Richard the next, and find in the doing of both, a common fulfillment. If acting be the food of love, Deeter was saying in his somewhat florid way, let it nourish you; make it a fact of your daily experience. He meant to demonstrate the truth in the ordinary. "As you think and feel and function, so does acting become a part of your being."

## Cupid Strikes

During the middle of my third year at Dartmouth, because of my obsession with the theater I quit school and joined the Hedgerow organization.

Mother and Father were much upset that I should give up my academic education for the theater. My father had hoped I would become a rabbi, at which I told him bluntly, "No way in hell!"

He had told me his own story many times. In order to prepare for his bar mitzvah, and because there was no rabbi in Mechanicsburg, PA, my father spent a year of study with Rabbi Nathan Rosenau in Philadelphia. He always spoke warmly of "The Rabbi" and must have learned his lessons well, for he not only became a Bar Mitzvah but became interested in the rabbinate himself. He also befriended the Rabbi's son, William, who was close to father's age. William did become a rabbi and one of the leaders in the Reform Movement, serving on the Board of Governors of the Hebrew Union College where he had been trained, and President of the Central Conference of American Rabbis. It became a life - long friendship and I remember, with pleasure, going to Baltimore on numerous occasions with my father to visit Rabbi Rosenau and his family. William Rosenau had become Chief Rabbi at Oheb Shalom, a prestigious synagogue in Baltimore.

It was because of my father's association with Rabbi Rosenau that, in his heart of hearts, my father had wanted to be a Rabbi. He hoped that perhaps his son would fulfill that desire. But that was not going to happen. I headed for an acting career in Rose Valley at the Hedgerow, a theater conceived as an artistic rather than a commercial venture which is one of the reasons it attracted so many young people.

One of the attracted young persons was Barbara Scott, known as "Bobbie", age 16 going on 17. She worked costumes, the box, the works. (Working the box means being part of the stage crew, making sure the props and scenery are on stage at the right time.)

That summer of '31 we became enamored with each other. At the end of the summer I went back for my sophomore year at Dartmouth, and Bobbie, who had just finished high school, started her freshman year at Bennington College in Vermont in Bennington's first class. It didn't take me long to realize I was falling in love with this lovely creature.

Our courtship lasted for the next few years, with trips from Dartmouth to Bennington and summers at Hedgerow. It was on one of my trips to Bennington that I met Bobbie's relative and roommate, Barbara Saul who, many years later would play a definitive role in my life.

By my junior year I knew Bobbie was the girl I was going to marry. Bobbie was back home in Rose Valley, having dropped out of school at the end of her sophomore year. Sadly, her father, Henry J. Scott, had lost everything in The Depression and had died, so she could no longer afford her schooling. Bobbie was offered a loan by the administration but refused it, not wanting to go into debt. She returned home to help her mother who had set up a boarding house for students from the Curtis Institute of Music in order to defray expenses.

One such boarder was Agnes Davis who, after graduating from Curtis, became an Opera star and sang leading roles with Mario Lanza. Another was Russian born Irra Petina, who became an actress and singer. At the Met, Patina was a leading contralto and critic Ken Mandelbaum referred to her as the "floperetta queen." In later years, she was a costar in Leonard Bernstein's *Candide*.

Rose Valley was a unique community. It was one of the smallest and wealthiest boroughs in the greater Philadelphia area, boasting that it had no stop lights, no sidewalks and no police force. Besides the Hedgerow Theater and a house belonging to the Pew Charitable Trust family, three other homes in Rose Valley had great significance to me. Across the street from the Theater was the Maurice Saul's stately mansion, surrounded by a complex of many buildings with a fine tennis court and a large swimming pool. Maurice Saul had established the prestigious law firm of Saul, Ewing, Remick and Saul and was known to his associates as "The Boss." The Sauls had two children, Barbara and Robert. Although it was Barbara Saul Sprogell whom I would marry after the death of Bobbie, our contact while at Hedgerow was limited. Barbara, who was in her teens, was sent to Paris to study piano with Nadia Boulanger for a year. Ms. Boulanger was considered one of the greatest teachers of the 20th century. Among her famous students were Aaron Copeland, Roy Harris, Leonard Bernstein and Virgil Thomson. She was also a longtime friend of Igor Stravinsky. Barbara must have had a great deal of talent to be allowed to study with such a famous piano teacher.

But it was her brother Robert whom I got to know best, for my friend and fellow-actor, Van Heflin, would play tennis with Robert on his family's tennis court which was across the street from Hedgerow.

Since I had some journalism experience in Harrisburg writing and editing on a Sunday paper under the watchful eye of Gus Steinmetz, plus doing the same for the Dartmouth daily paper, Deeter assigned me to publicity to coincide with my acting.

There were six newspapers in Philadelphia in the early 1930s and I, as the Hedgerow Theater's publicist, made the rounds every Tuesday to give the drama editors and reporters an update on what was playing at the Hedgerow. I got to know these well-informed newspaper men and women and also quickly learned the best route to follow, allowing me to see them all in one day.

Starting downtown, I hit the *Ledger*. It was the only paper in town that published a morning and evening edition so I had to make sure I caught both the AM and PM theatrical editors, Arthur Waters, H.T. Murdock and Richard Powell. Richard later became a novelist and wrote *"The Young Philadelphians,"* which, in 1959, was made into a movie staring Paul Newman. My next stop was Filbert and Juniper Streets to contact R. P. Senderfer and Paul Cranston at the *Bulletin*. Then it was up Broad Street to The *Record* where David Stern, the son of the owner, and Hobe Morrison worked. Hobe later moved to New York as editor of *Variety's* "legit" section. "Legit," a contraction of the word legitimate, means it only covered plays, no vaudeville or burlesque. Walking across the street to The *Inquirer* I'd stop in to see Lawrence Davis, the bureau chief. The New York *Times* kept its out-of-town bureau in the Inquirer building and Linton Martin and his wife, Helen, were there along with Sam Singer, their assistant. I have to chuckle; Sam became deaf later in life and was put on the complaint desk to handle all those nasty calls. Can you imagine? It was "yes, ma'am; no, ma'am; I am terribly sorry for your inconvenience" and he never heard a word of the complaint.

Last stop was the *Daily News* at 22$^{nd}$ and Arch Streets where Jeff Keen and then Gerry Gaghan, after Keen retired, hung out. I knew all these guys from my early twenties. I was getting my feet wet as a press agent. At night I became an actor. I was also planning to get married in June to my true love, Bobbie Scott.

It was while I was at Hedgerow that I first met Brooks Atkinson, the drama critic for the New York *Times*. Al Hirschfeld, the famous artist for the *Times,* drove Brooks down to the Hedgerow to review various shows. Brooks didn't drive and Al loved to even though the ninety miles from New York, on US Route 1, was long and arduous. In those days turnpikes were still on the drawing board. Our meeting marked the start of a long friendship between the three of us.

Brooks returned to Hedgerow often, staying with his nephew, Tyson Peabody, who was an attorney for The Scott Paper Company. Often I would see Brooks with binoculars at the ready, birding on Ridley Creek behind the Hedgerow where the stream winds its way to the Delaware River.

*Married at 23*

On June 14th, 1935, Bobbie and I were married in the Quaker tradition at the home of Mildred Olmsted, Bobbie's step-sister, in Rose Valley. Mildred's living room lent itself to the wedding which was just a small family affair.

We chose Quakerism because Bobbie, coming from a Scottish Protestant background, and I, from a German Jewish one, thought the Quaker philosophy and religion was a good meeting ground for both of us.

Even though the wedding was beautiful and my bride looked radiant in her gorgeous wedding suit, it was bittersweet for me because my parents were not in attendance. They let me know that they thoroughly disapproved of our marriage. I was marrying out of the faith; Bobbie was not Jewish, I was marrying a "shiksa."

If you can believe it, on my wedding morning I received a call from my parents who tried to dissuade me from going through with the ceremony. But the crowning blow came from my mother when she wailed, "Children have been stoned for less." I was disowned by my own family.

We honeymooned for a weekend in Red Bank, NJ and stayed at the Molly Pitcher Hotel. I picked that hotel because I had played the town and liked the hotel.

Relations did not improve with my parents once we were married. When Bobbie and I went to Harrisburg for a visit, my parents treated Bobbie as if she were a ghost, refusing to speak to her. You can imagine how my 21 year-old young bride felt; she was deeply hurt, as was I.

It was difficult for me to understand my parents' reaction to my new marital status. I had always been, in their eyes, the perfect son. I had done well in school and was president of my senior class, so my contemporaries must have approved of me; my grades in school were always exemplary; the reports my parents received from teachers were always positive and noted leadership qualities. I had succeeded in becoming an Eagle Scout. I had even won the American Legion medal for outstanding leadership when I was a counselor at the Boy Scout Camp in Loysville, PA

So, why did they want to cut themselves off from their only son? I know they thoroughly disapproved of my not finishing college and I knew only too well their reluctance to take my Christian wife to their bosom. But let me say this; the joy that came with my first year of marriage was certainly dampened by my lack of relations with my parents.

Fortunately, as the year progressed, the ice thawed a bit, and at least there was communication between the newlyweds and the senior Jacobsons.

But it wasn't until February of '36 that I began to understand what was motivating my parents. For over twenty years their only son, a quiet and shy youngster, had conformed to most of their demands. Now that he was married the control didn't work. As a married couple, Bobbie and I wanted to strike out on our own, make our own decisions, pick an employment that suited me, and live the life of our dreams.

I had just returned from a second tour with The Hedgerow Players. My wife was five months pregnant and I was well aware that I needed a paying job to support my family. Continuing with Hedgerow was not in the equation.

The February letters below, one addressed to both of us, the other just to Barbara (Bobbie), are very revealing.

*Feb 19ᵗʰ, 1936*

*My Dears:-*

*Not having heard a word from you since Sol's return, I grew concerned and called up Hedgerow at eleven o'clock last night and am sorry that I could not talk to you. Today I received your letters to mother* *and Uncle Dave. Your balance in the bank is $ 441.70. Whilst your income is shrinking annually due to poorer returns on your investments, you need not worry too much as there is in your savings account here over $4300 which is bringing in about $100 a year that can be transferred to your account as needed. I need not add that you always have a home at 2129 and in our hearts. Dwelling there need not imply working at the Kuhn Clothing Co. but can always be to you a refuge as long as we exist.*

*I agree with your mother this part of the letter is addressed more particularly to your Barbara. Before the expected event, will you please look after that other baby that was once mine and is now yours. See that his neck and ears are kept properly clean. He, early in life, showed his artistic temperament by an aversion to keeping those somewhat conspicuous parts of his anatomy as clean as social environments demand and Hedgerow did nothing to change his ideas on that subject. His clothes, too, must need replenishing and care. Please see that he gets what he needs and draw on me for anything except shoes and hats. Those you must buy in Philadelphia. or Media or wherever you shop. Is his overcoat heavy enough in this severe weather? If not, let me know at once and I will send him one. The best I can do so late in the season.*

*Sorry to have to appear so officious in theses purely personal matters but Sol has not yet learned that the world is not so indifferent in these matters as he is. It is up to*

*you to teach him. I was too incompetent and
too impatient to do it myself. Must close now
with love to you both,*

> *Sincerely,*
> *Dad*

*Feb 27th, 1936*

*My Barbara:-*

    *In accordance with your letter, I sent
Sol four shirts which I hope will please you
both. In lieu of any other address I sent them
care of Hedgerow. If you do not receive
them between now and Saturday, let me
know and I'll put a tracer on them. I hope
Soly got back alright and that he landed a
job. Young men no longer look for a position
– just a job. In case he does not, I think it
would be wise for you to come here and look
around. This does not mean that he should
come to the store. If he wants to take a try at
the business that will be up to him as I never
tried to influence him in that direction. I can
only say he could do worse. Dear mother is
coming home in a few hours and I hope to
find her in good health and spirits. Sorry the
two of you could not get down to see her.*
    *Love to you both, keep well,*

> *Dad*

## *The Hedgerow Bus and Truck Tour*

I was still working at the Hedgerow Theater, making plans to go with the "Hedgerow Players" on a tour. It was a tough, time-consuming assignment and I would be away from my newlywed wife for months, but that's show business and, in 1935, in the middle of the Depression, I was fortunate to have any job.

So at the age of 23 and just married I, with 14 others, piled into an old parochial school bus and, with a new Dodge truck filled with stage settings and props, we headed to the Midwest and became the first "Traveling Bus and Truck Drama Group" in the United States. When I could, I tried my best to travel in the Truck, a much more comfortable ride than the old School bus, which really was a kidney shaker.

Our trip was booked by Lucius Pryor, of Council Bluffs, Iowa and Richard Bridges of Atlanta, our managers. They arranged for our troupe to play in universities all through the Midwest with housing accommodations at the local hotels.

Weeks before our trip began and ahead of our appearances I prepared a press book and a photo kit to distribute to the universities.

We started in Council Bluffs, with a free performance at the local high school where our booking manager, Lucius Pryor lived and had children in school. We then dropped South, hitting Nebraska, Kansas, Oklahoma, Texas, Louisiana and Mississippi, ending up in Daytona, Florida. Our longest stays were for a week in Iowa City, Iowa, Stillwater, Oklahoma, and Chapel Hill, North Carolina at their respective universities. Playwright-professor Paul Green, whose *In Abraham's Bosom* Deeter had staged for the Provincetown Playhouse, was our host at the Carolina Playmakers at the University of North Carolina in Chapel Hill. Another distinguished professor, Archibald Henderson, who was head of the mathematics department and Bernard Shaw's first biographer, tossed a party for us. We had many Shaw plays in our repertory. Professor Henderson became our advisor when Hedgerow launched the first Shaw Festival the following year. In all, we traveled over five thousand miles.

The Hedgerow Players were a repertory theater group and our eclectic repertoire included Shakespeare's *12th Night* and *Roadside* by Lynn Riggs better known for his play *Green Grow the Lilacs* which, incidentally, many years later became Rodgers and Hammerstein's musical, *Oklahoma.*.

All of us did a little of everything; however, I was beginning to find that publicity was more to my liking than acting even though I had perfected an excellent Scottish accent as a character actor. While at the Hedgerow I had acted in *Angus,* a Gilbert (of Gilbert and Sullivan) play. I had a two-liner. In my finest Scottish accent, wearing a kilt, I'd say, " Twa pon is twa pon" which, translated, meant "two pounds is two pounds." But my accent really flourished when I imitated the famous Scottish comedian, Harry Lauder.

There were no super highways in those days, and our travel was slow along country roads, through small and large towns. However, because of the distance we had to travel, we all had to drive the vehicles at one time or another. Driving classes were given but somehow, unfortunately, I missed them: I was too busy putting up signs and talking with editors of the university newspapers. So, when it came to be my turn, forward gear was fine but reverse was anathema to me.

The only real excitement of the trip was when we hit a cow in Oklahoma. The cow mistook the roadway for a pasture and we barreled into the poor beast. Fortunately the dumb animal was able to get up and we chased it back into the pasture. I'm afraid it was more scared than hurt, as were we. No, I was not driving.

It was tough being away from Bobbie but the phone had been invented and the US mail service was very much in business. On one such call I heard, to my great joy, that my wife was pregnant.

I didn't want to share this good news with others because I tried to keep my private life separate. I knew I would be leaving the Hedgerow soon after my return; now that I was a married man, I needed a paying job.

Later, during my trip through the West, I decided that acting was not for me, even though I had acted in over 200 plays at Hedgerow, with the novelty of a rotating repertoire, where it would be a Spewack play one night, a Synge comedy or a Lennox Robinson play the next. After two college summers as a night time actor and later as a daytime press agent, I decided that being a publicist was for me. Preparing press books and laying out a campaign that took the Hedgerow Theater and its press agent-actor into 20 Midwestern and Southern States were what I enjoyed. It made me aware that I was better at pounding the typewriter than I was at playing an actor's role. I also learned that the trip we had just finished with Hedgerow players had never been done before as a school bus and truck tour. It was considered ground-breaking.

Jasper Deeter, my boss and a fine actor-director had the belief that all great actors shared a necessary ingredient, "a prejudice on their own behalf." My prejudice was that saying the lines someone else wrote night after night was not for me.

In the five years I spent at Hedgerow, the most significant event for me was my creation of the George Bernard Shaw Festival, which I started on

July 26, in 1934, to coincide with G.B.S.'s birthday. For two weeks, Hedgerow would schedule six of Shaw's plays in rotation, *Arms and The Man, The Devil's Disciple, Androcles and the Lion, You Never Can Tell, Heartbreak House* and *Saint Joan,* a different one every night. It was one of the first such events in North America.

Well known authors like Theodore Dreiser and Sherwood Anderson came to Hedgerow to take up temporary residence while Deeter staged *An American Tragedy* and *Winesburg, Ohio.*

Among the actors in my time who went on to Broadway or Hollywood were John Beal, whose most notable screen appearance was in *Les Misérables* (1935); his wife Helen Craig, who worked steadily in early films, TV and stage; Richard Basehart, one of whose most notable film roles was the acrobat known as "The Fool" in the acclaimed Italian film *La Strada* directed by Federico Fellini (Basehart was also known for his deep, distinctive voice and was prolific as a narrator of many television and movie projects ranging from features to documentaries); Allyn Joslyn, who was on stage from age 17 and played a leading man in *Boy Meets Girl*(1936) and *Arsenic and Old Lace* (1941), appearing in the latter as beleaguered theatrical critic Mortimer Brewster; and Van Heflin, who played mostly character parts as a leading man over the course of his film career. Van Heflin won the Academy Award for Best Supporting Actor for his performance in *Johnny Eager* (1942).

Many marriages, I counted 28 of them, were forged at Hedgerow, including my own to Barbara Scott and, after her death, to Barbara Saul Sprogell.

*My first paying jobs*

How could I desert the world of Art for the "Markets of Commerce?" For one thing, Bobbie was going to have a baby, and for another, living communally while being married was hardly an overwhelming pleasure. Privacy was scarce, and, to me, a rare commodity, especially in the Hedgerow Theater group.

So, I turned in my part-books and took my scrapbook, my bride and my hopes to the nearest town, Philadelphia, and with regret I left Rose Valley. It had been a great education, especially those two tours with The Hedgerow Players through the Midwest and South.

Mildred Scott Olmsted, Bobbie's aunt, suggested I work as publicist for her organization, The Women's International League for Peace and Freedom. They were sponsoring a theater series, *The Clare Tree Major Series*. My employment lasted only a few months and I felt I had not been very effective. Mildred then recommended me for a job with the American Friends Service Committee. There I worked in their publicity department doing stories for local area papers regarding the AFS Peace Caravans. These Caravans were of young college folks, backed by local church groups, who were sent out into the community to hold seminars on alternate ways to head off World War II, which was obviously coming in Europe.

In 1936, the lives of the Jewish people in Germany were becoming intolerable as the resounding anti-Semitic rhetoric increased. The Service Committee wasn't blowing their horn about it, but along with the Peace Caravans, AFSC was also trying to rescue Jews, at that time, from the Hitler regime. And they were being listened to by the powers-to-be because of the successful Quaker feeding programs in Germany after World War I.

They say that the birth of a child is a miracle but, for me, it was a double miracle.

Judy was born on June 10$^{th}$, 1936 and, T.G., her birth made peace in the family. Mother and Dad relented in their objections to Bobbie and my father went out of his way to reunite the family.

My Dad's letter is proof:

*July 4th, 1936*

*Dear Sol and Barbara:-*

*The high spot in your birthday celebra-*
*tion was your consent to have darling Judith*

44

*named in the faith to which she was born. She is now my grand-daughter rather than my offspring. I hope that you do not think me a religious fanatic. You know I am not. I am just a human being with all the failings and weakness of my fellowman. I am though, especially now when our people are going through such terrible straits, intensely Jewish and it behooves every one of us to stand up loyally for our faith and our ideals. I am happy to think that my son will not fail us in this respect. You are now parents and I am sure realize all the hopes and aspirations that go with parenthood. Enough on this subject. I shall not afflict you further with my views on this subject or any other for that matter as I like you to make up your minds for yourselves.*

*I quite agree that you should keep Mrs. Hopkinson longer as Barbara can not be strong enough to carry on all the housework and look after Judith, too.*

*Your balance in the bank July $2^{nd}$, with a check of $307.00 just deposited, is $499.61. Don't worry about the financial end of your life. You know the little we have is yours and, as long as I can take care of my business, there will be sufficient for all of our needs.*

*Uncle Dave tells me that if you do not cash that check he sent you, it will merely be making a present to the bank as it was a treasurer's check and not his own. So don't be foolish. Don't forget it adds to our happiness to help provide for your comfort and well being.*

*For your sake I hope you will land a congenial position and in a measure be self supporting. Sol Kuhn once said, "Success in business adds nothing to a man's character and failure takes nothing from it." This is true but it does add a lot to your self respect if you can feel that you are standing on your own feet and that is why I am anxious that you get started in some gainful occupation.*

*Your devotion to Barbara and Judith and Barbara's devotion to you make me very happy. It is in the true tradition of the Jacobson spirit. I may beat your mother but "Gawd how I luv her".*

*I am anxiously looking forward to the 12th to see you all especially our dear granddaughter. I expect to see a great improvement in her and hope to hear the music of her voice. Love to you and kindest remembrances from your mother.*

*Dad*

We rented a not-so-nice furnished apartment at 15th and Market. Fortunately, my employment with AFSC was also short-lived because in the fall, Samuel Nixon-Nirdlinger came to my rescue taking me on as "house agent" for the Erlanger Theatre. My mother in-law, Jessalyn Scott, a newly proud Grandma, was a friend of Sam's and his wife Jane, told them of my success as publicist with Hedgerow. "He knows all the editors of all the Philadelphia newspapers and I believe you would be well served if you hired my son-in-law, Sol."

After I landed the job we moved from Market Street to 1630 Locust, to a much nicer apartment. It was a furnished flat on the first floor of a brownstone. From our Locust Street apartment we could easily wheel baby Judy, in her baby carriage, to Rittenhouse Square where we spent many delightful hours feeding the pigeons and enjoying the Fall colors. But even better, Bobbie's mother had moved to the Touraine Apartments around the corner, where we could park Judy for the night. Not only a built in babysitter but the price was right.

Sam had recently been made manager of the vast playhouse that Ziegfeld and Abraham Lincoln Erlanger had built in the late twenties at Market and 22$^{nd}$ Streets. Before the Nixon take over nobody had used the building; it was standing idle, unused.

This Georgian structure had been the pride of the U.S. The interior was furnished in the Napoleonic French style. It boasted three lobbies, the grand stairs and many lounges. The auditorium seated 1,890 and was elaborately decorated with imported marble, gold leaf, murals, tapestries, and crystal chandeliers. It was the most elaborate legitimate theater ever built in the United States.

During the Depression it had fallen into the hands of the First Pennsylvania Company which held the mortgage and considered it a white elephant. Tommy LaBrum, who had publicized the Nixon interests for Sam's father and for Sam, had declined to work for the scion of the family any longer. Perhaps it had been over salaries or that he just wanted to go out on his own, building his own agency. Whatever, I was offered LaBrum's job. Tommy was a model of what is needed as a local area publicist and I knew it would be a hard act to follow.

Tommy worked for the Nixon-Nirdlinger chain, which was always second best to the mighty Shubert Empire. He was a member of a prominent Philadelphia family, some of which pronounced their name with the accent on the second syllable while others on the first. Tommy, a perennial bachelor, always sported a striking beauty on his arm as he walked down Chestnut Street. In introducing her to me he would say "My Cousin, kid," as he sauntered into the lobby for an opening. At one of his openings he would post himself by the press agent or manager and introduce key people to them as they filed in. He was a tower of strength. Turkey or hit, everyone wanted Tommy LaBrum on their side. Tommy could have made it to Broadway any time he chose and was asked to do so by the producer actor George M. Cohan. But Tommy much preferred the Main Line and his own pace to the frenetic competition of New York City. He was quite content being an advisor to the Stern interests at the *Record*, and running the Salvation Army's annual campaign along with being a press agent. He knew every reporter, editor, linotypist, and pressman in Philly. And whenever a show needed "to paper" the house so as to assure the actors a sounding board, Tommy was your man.

Tommy built a very successful Philadelphia public relations firm and we became very good friends. His agency did all kinds of publicity for a variety of events rather than specializing just in the theater. Even though his agency was successful, I'll never forget his advice; "Sol," he said, "if you want to be successful as a press agent in the theater, New York City is the place to be. That's where the action is. I was given that opportunity once and turned it down. George M. Cohan had asked me to be his agent. Don't make the same mistake I made."

I took these words of wisdom to heart and after a summer in New Hampshire followed by a stint at the Erlanger, I went to New York City and landed a job with The Shubert organization in 1937 for a little more than a year.

Then to George Abbott as an associate press agent, thanks to the good offices of Phyllis Perlman who was Abbott's publicist. Curiously enough, three years later, in the summer of 1940, I would be working for Phyllis's husband, Theron Bamberger, as press agent when he took over the management of the Bucks County Playhouse in New Hope, PA. But, I'm getting ahead of myself; let's go back to Sam Nixon at the Erlanger.

A show that is bound for Broadway is usually tried out in one or more cities, giving the producer the opportunity to tighten the script, change a dance routine, and rewrite a song or whatever is needed. There is nothing like a live audience to inform the producer if he is on the right track or how to correct it if he is not.

Three to four weeks before an opening in a tryout city, the show's advance man or press agent arrives to work the publicity for the show. It is the duty of the local house agent to assist in this venture. The house agent has the advantage of knowing the newspaper editors in the city and can be a conduit for the out-of-town press agent to get his story in the paper and subsequently to the public.

The likes of *Tobacco Road* on its third time around, and various and sundry attractions that were not going to the Shubert House in New York, wandered into the Erlanger. We were not considered a Philadelphia first run theater; many times we booked mediocre shows along with some real losers. As house agent, I received a salary only when an attraction was in the house, which unfortunately, while I was with the Erlanger was less frequent than I would have liked.

However, there was a more positive side. Little did I know that Bill Doll and Lewis Harmon, whom I would meet that season at the Erlanger, would shape the rest of my working days.

Bill Doll was a breezy lad from West Virginia who had recently taken over from Barclay McCarthy as Alex Yokel's publicist in New York City. McCarthy had gone on to Hollywood and Warner Brothers to work on Yokel's goldmine, *Three Men on a Horse*, about to be released on film.

Bill brought the show, a mystery thriller called *Love from a Stranger,* to the Erlanger for a tryout. The show had just gone into rehearsal in New York and, after interviewing his British cast, many of whom had just gotten off the trans-Atlantic steamer the day before, Bill hurried off to Philadelphia.

Mr. Doll had the phenomenal ability to write his whole campaign on my battered typewriter, staying up the entire night and then carrying the copy around to the newspapers with me the next morning. In later years, he would become a partner in my own agency, called Doll, Harmon and Jacobson.

The second influence was Alex Yokel's nephew, Lewis Harmon, who was also Yokel's company manager. Louis was about my age, a former publicist for Ziegfeld. He, too, would join me and Bill as a partner in my agency.

The third was then and throughout his entire lifetime, Broadway's busiest and most prodigious publicist, Richard Sylvester Maney. This Irishman, who was born in Montana and educated in Seattle, came to Philadelphia as a publicist for John C. Wilson's *Excursion*, a slight fantasy about a Staten Island ferryboat captain who goes to sea, authored by Victor Wolfson. It had a good cast including Whitford Kane, Shirley Booth, and others.

In the Spring of 1937, Maney, who disdained spending a night away from his beloved New York, breezed in and out of Philadelphia in a day, leaving such distinctive copy about the play, *Excursion*, behind him as few editors had ever read.

Years later I became an associate of this beguiling, delightful human being, spending days in his drafty quarters above the Empire Theater's marquee on Broadway, opposite the old Metropolitan Opera. All of us who ever worked with this literate, lovable man felt the same about him. No amount of money could compensate for the zany, wonderful years with Maney. God knows, Richard Sylvester wasn't everyone's cup of tea. His irreverence shook the stuffing out of many, particularly those who fancied their own importance. But if you valued integrity combined with a saving wit, Maney was your man. He certainly was my "man for all seasons."

## Summer in New Hampshire

It was through a friend of the Hedgerow Theater that I obtained my summer job of 1936. Beatrice Beach McCloud was head of the drama department at Swarthmore College and one of the founding members of the "49ers," a group of graduates from the Yale Drama School who established the Chase Barn Playhouse, in Whitefield, NH, a summer theater.

Chase Barn Playhouse, Whitefield, N. H.

Was I interested in being their publicity agent? That was an understatement; we were right in the middle of America's worst depression. At 24, I jumped at the opportunity.

Bill Chase, a bachelor and the legendary music editor of the New York *Times*, had inherited from his family a large farm outside of Whitefield. So, when the group was looking for a home for their theater, philanthropist Bill stepped forward and offered them his barn. As seen in the picture from an old postal card, a stage was set up in front of rows of chairs, 13 wide by 10 deep. Extra chairs on the right and left allowed 175 theater-goers to enjoy the show. If you look closely at the photo, you'll notice that half the chairs have plush, soft seats that are embroidered.

INTERIOR OF_ CHASE BARN PLAYHOUSE_ WHITEFIELD, N. H.

Previous to the opening of the theater, Bill Chase received a call from his good friend Bill Guarne, press agent for the Metropolitan Opera.

"Would you like some fancy chairs for your new theater?" he asked Bill. "The Met is getting new chairs and the old ones are going begging". "Certainly," was Chase's answer, and within a few days, the chairs arrived, thanks to the Metropolitan's truck.

Bill Chase was a man with a heart of gold. It is said that one day while walking the streets of New York in midwinter, he came upon a beggar shivering in the cold. Warm hearted Bill took off his overcoat and gave it to him.

Whitefield was an ideal place for a summer theater. Nestled in the White Mountain National Forest, ten miles north of the Presidential Range, Whitefield offered not only the mountains but the clear, cool breezes of summer. It became a favorite summer vacation spot for those who loved theater and dreaded the hot and sticky pavements of the big city. The Mountain View Inn of Whitefield, run by the Dodge Brothers, catered to this group, serving them good food, good wine and spectacular views of the Presidential Range.

My job was traveling the State, putting up posters, planting stories about what was showing, and meeting the editors of the local newspapers. We were lucky; our theater flourished despite the tough times. Perhaps I had something to do with their success, who knows. But the great break for me was to mix with, and get to know, many of the New York newspaper people such as Neil McNeil, managing editor of the New York *Times*, Howard Taubman, music editor, who later became drama critic for The *Times* and Frank Perkins, musical editor of the *Herald Tribune*. They were all guests of Bill at the farm. I, too, stayed in one of the cottages on the farm, along with my whole family.

Bobbie worked in the box office with baby Judy in her bassinette right beside her. You can imagine the oohs and aahs she received from the theater goers. Charles Evans Hughes, Chief Justice of the Supreme Court and his wife were among those admirers. I remember the Chief Justice well because he always looked the part. He was an impressive figure with full mustache, heavy eyebrows and a well trimmed beard. It was his wife who used to say, "I really came to see the baby, not the show."

In the Fall of '36, when I became an associate agent in New York City, these contacts that I had made in Whitefield were extremely helpful to me, giving me a leg-up in the industry. They might not have remembered me but they surely remembered my cute little baby.

# ACT II

★ ★ ★

## *My Early Career on Broadway*

## *My first job in New York, New York*

Bill Doll, Lou Harmon and Tommy LaBraum had all suggested that I give up Philadelphia and try my luck in New York as a press agent, for, as they put it, "That's where the action is." With that in mind, I took my leave from Whitefield, N.H. for a few days in August to see what might be available. Wrong move; I got nowhere. It was hot mid-summer in New York City and my contacts were either on vacation or not interested.

In 1936, when I came to New York City looking for a job as a publicist after my summer in Whitefield, Ray Henderson was the soul of kindness. I was a kid of 24 and he asked me to come to his office to see how he could help me. Busy as he was, once in his inner sanctum he stopped everything and gave his full attention to my request for employment. Without hesitation, he picked up his phone and arranged an appointment for me with the Shuberts' general press representative, C.P. Greneker. He had heard that Greneker, the Shuberts' publicist, had just transferred one of his associate press agents to another department where he felt she, Ms. Freeman, would be more effective. That left an opening to fill. This is what I heard Ray say to C.P: "Alas, I have no need of an associate, but the Shuberts have many productions in the works; perhaps you can use this fine young man." These few words to C.P. Greneker from a well-respected fellow publicist were the only introduction I needed. After hanging up the phone, Ray turned to me and said, "Go get the job," and I did.

Ray was born in Colorado Springs, Colorado. He was so stage-struck that he became an extra at Elitch's Garden, Denver's noted Summer Theater. After that he served as a box-office man in Colorado Springs, where he was persuasive enough to get himself hired as a theater reviewer for a daily newspaper. It was the San Francisco Italian Opera Company that got him started as a press agent.

When Henderson died in a seaplane crash in the Bay of Athens in 1937 at the age of 48, he had already been Katharine Cornell's press agent for seven and a half years. He was the most respected and admired press agent in America and the president of the New York Theatrical Press Agents Association which had been formed the year before. As Richard Maney, a fellow flugler (another name for a press agent), wrote in The Sunday *Herald Tribune*, "Ray Henderson was something more than the first press agent. He was one of the first gentlemen of the American Theater."

I had met Henderson when I was a neophyte press agent for the Hedgerow Theater in the spring of 1934. He came to town to publicize Katharine Cornell's production of Shaw's *Saint Joan.* Henderson was Cornell's press agent on tour.

I got to know Ray because I was the one who had the pleasure of schlepping him around to see the editors of our Philadelphia newspapers. And then, of course, we had to have lunch, so we had the chance to know each other even better.

As long as I knew Ray he was Katharine Cornell's devoted publicist. It has been reported that when Guthrie McClintic, Katharine Cornell's husband (their marriage was always described as a "lavender" marriage, for both were gay) got the bright notion to engage Henderson for Miss Cornell in 1931, Ray was well known to both of them. As far back as 1917, when Katharine was playing with the Washington Square Players, Henderson had been dispatched by his friend, William Faversham, the legendary English actor who had starred as Algernon in the original production of *The Importance of Being Earnest,* to see her perform in *Plots and Playwrights,* a comedy by Edward Massey. Ray reported favorably not only to Faversham but also to Cornell's father, Doc Cornell, who was manager of the Star Theater in Buffalo. To both he related, "Miss Cornell has a future in the theater; she conducted herself like a professional."

Henderson, from the first, began his national barrage of publicity for the "First Lady of the Theater." He never used that phrase but saw to it that the editors did. He was not only a superb publicity man for both Miss Cornell and McClintic, but a trusted friend and adviser whose counsel was sought on many business matters as well.

*Katharine Cornell - signed photo to Judy*
*"To Judy - Best Wishes – Katharine Cornell"*

Ray was a stickler when it came to the spelling of Miss Cornell's first name, "Katharine." He sent post cards to the editors' desks along with his articles, hoping the proof readers would read them. The postcard carried the legend; "Why her name is spelled Katharine." And it read, "The second "a" in Miss Cornell's spelling of her first name has tempted Tories of feminine nomenclature to accuse her of affectation. It happens, however, that they are wrong and she is right in spite of the fact that the common English spelling is Katherine or Catherine. Miss Cornell, as a Katharine, is on sounder ground than any of her old-fashioned namesakes, for she is using the Greek spelling of early martyroligists. Saint Katharine of Alexandria, earliest of the six canonized Kates, popularized the name, in its many forms, for all of Christendom."

It was Ray who conceived the idea of the 1933-1934 Cornell tour with a repertory of three plays. That was quite an innovative and risky concept in those mid-depression days considering that half the Broadway theaters were closed due to the lack of paying customers. But Ray was adamant, and was convinced the tour would be successful. They chose three plays for the tour; *The Barretts of Wimpole Street* by Rudolph Besier, *Candida* by George Bernard Shaw and Shakespeare's *Romeo and Juliet,* which would star Miss Cornell. Her husband, Guthrie McClintic, would be the producer.

The tour was a booming success. The 17,000 miles and 225 performances in 34 states set box office records. And it inspired other Broadway stars to emulate Miss Cornell.

Henderson's work was brilliant. He not only kept up a local tattoo of communiqués ahead of the show, usually three weeks in advance, but sent communiqués across the nation. By dint of hard, professional work he alerted the entire country to the prodigious work of his star. The human interest copy that poured out of the Cornell tour was inspiring, and eagerly sought by drama editors. When the performance in Seattle, McClintic's home town, was delayed until after 2 AM because of torrential washouts on the railroads, the sellout audience that Christmas Night at the Metropolitan Theater remained in their seats. It was a tribute to the star's reputation and magnetism, and that delay became an often repeated story, part of the Broadway lore. Everyone working in the theater, from the highest to the lowest, felt ennobled by Cornell and the legends that Henderson helped create.

One of the actors in *The Barretts of Wimpole Street* was a cocker spaniel named Flush who not only played his part as *Elizabeth Barrett's* pet but was also Miss Cornell's delightful traveling companion as she toured the country. Thanks to Ray's publicity, everyone knew about Flush and he became a star in his own right. And as for the hotels that did not permit travelers to bring their pets, they were put on a black list, never to be visited again.

When the tour ended, Ray relaxed by heading for Europe, dreaming of an even mightier tour. This time it was to be a global one. He broached it to Guthrie McClintic and Miss Cornell. They were interested but it would be in the planning stage for three years.

In 1937, Ray went on an exploratory trip. His letters, cables and phone calls were enthusiastic. Henderson showed that the project "was logically feasible and financially practicable." Even Bali and Java had been visited. Ray's last cable had been from Cairo to Miss Kit at her Martha's Vineyard home; "Egypt keen. Flying London tomorrow."

The next day, October 2, 1937, McClintic and his secretary, Miss Macy, arrived in New York to receive the bad news. At the same time Ray's cable was being delivered at the Vineyard to Miss Cornell, the U.S. consulate in Athens cabled her New York Office; "Henderson trapped and drowns in submerged seaplane." Only three passengers seated in the front of the cabin were killed. They were buried immediately in Athens.

Ray, who was beloved by all who worked with him, was deeply mourned up and down Broadway but most especially by actress Lillian Gish. Miss Gish, then starring in a McClintic production of Maxwell Anderson's *The Star Wagon* at the Empire Theater, wanted Ray's body returned to the United States for an American burial. Since the body could not be exhumed and returned to the United States unless personally escorted, Miss Gish arranged, through a friend, to bring Henderson's body home on an Italian liner. Cremation followed, and as Ray had directed in his will, his brother had his remains scattered over his beloved Rocky Mountains at Pike's Peak, overlooking his hometown.

My favorite photograph of Ray used to hang in the box office of the Empire Theater until the day that historic house was leveled. I used to pop in there in the days I worked upstairs with Dick Maney, just to see my old friend. The photo showed the laughing publicist with Lillian Gish seated on his lap. A press photographer had snapped it on stage at a party celebrating the McClintic production of *Hamlet* which had achieved a record run in New York. John Gielgud was the star with Miss Gish as his Ophelia. That was the Ray Henderson who had arranged the interview that now sent me to the Sardi Building.

# Scene *2*

## C.P. Greneker and the Shuberts

I made sure I was on time for my interview with C.P. Greneker, getting there a little early. I was dressed in my tweed jacket and Daks slacks, my usual British fashion attire thanks to my wife who purchased all my clothes. Years ago, as a youngster, I worked in my father's clothing store during the holidays. I detested the experience. It was not for me and I made the decision that, if and when I got married, my wife would always purchase my clothes. Fortunately, Bobbie learned what sizes I needed. She would try on a jacket that she thought would be right, knowing that the sleeve should extend so many inches from her hand. The pants were sized and were OK around the middle, but usually had to be re-cuffed in length. In the years that followed, I never set foot into a men's clothing store; it was a rule that I never broke.

The Shuberts' press department was sequestered on the third floor of Sardi's Restaurant and looked more like a pawn shop than an office. Lord knows it was not famous for its beauty, but never mind, I was in New York City, employed right smack in the heart of Broadway. If I needed luxury all I had to do was look up at the sixth floor where J.J. Shubert had his penthouse apartment or at his brother Lee's apartment across the street. Although both of them helped run the Shubert Empire, I learned only too quickly that they didn't speak to each other.

Think of it. In my mid-twenties I was hoping to become, along with Samuel J. Friedman and Lewis Friedman, an associate press agent for the Shuberts' in New York City. Yes!

At the appointed hour I was ushered into C.P. Greneker's inner sanctum. Claude P. Greneker, had been head of the Shuberts' press department for many years and did most of the press agent hiring and firing for the many attractions that the Messrs. Lee and J.J., and cousin Milton, presented. He looked and acted the part of a cool southern gentleman.

As I entered "Grennie's" (as C.P. Greneker was known in the trade) office I noticed his neat desk had two piles of envelopes which he had obviously separated before my arrival. One pile contained letters requesting free passes to Shubert shows while the other was self-addressed envelopes from those same optimistic seekers of free passes. Curiously, all through my interview he carefully removed the stamps from the self-addressed franked envelopes and placed them in a box. I guess he was trying to imply frugality comes with being a Shubert press agent.

After looking over my resume, Mr. Greneker wasted no time in saying, "You're hired. I'll introduce you to Sam Friedman tomorrow."

Samuel J. Friedman, a press agent on Broadway from the mid-thirties until the early 70's, was one of the most unusual publicists of his day, both in his volatile personality and his dedication to his profession. I would learn from him what a press agent should and should not do.

So, the next day C.P. introduced me to the other associate press agents, turning me over to Sam who would teach me the ropes. I also met Abner Klipstein, a smiling gnome just out of N.Y.U.'s School of Commerce, who officiated at a desk, sorting through piles of papers for C.P to summarize.

A brief tour of the office showed that there were glass partitions outside C.P.'s office and behind these were filing cabinets with 11" by 14" envelopes for photos, chiefly portraits in sepia of the players in the *Student Prince, Blossom Time*, or any of the other shows that made the Shubert Empire flourish at that time. Behind Greneker's office was a smaller one for his secretary of many years, Dora Upfland. At the back of her office was the bullpen which housed the associate press agents. That is where I would be working.

As soon as Sam discovered that I knew the rudiments of our trade, had been around the theater since I was knee high to the proverbial grasshopper, and that I had a wife and young baby to support, he hopped into action on my behalf.

"Here, write a story about this English character actor, Charles Donkin, who plays Frederick, the Principal of a boarding school in *Bachelor Born*. The 'Admiral,' (that's how we refer to Milton Shubert, our supreme leader), just brought this show over from England and it is due to open at the Morosco Theater. Make it three pages, double spaced. Here's the Playbill and the British Who's Who. And give me the article before lunch. I'll place it."

I did as Sam requested. Later, I learned that he had phoned Frank Farrell, the drama editor of the *World-Telegram*, told him C.P. had hired a new guy, Sol Jacobson, who needed a job badly. Would he please run the story soon. Sol would bring the article down along with a photo. Please forget the other Shubert shows and run this one.

The next day the World-Telegram carried the piece with a fine two column head, including the photo. Sam came into C.P.'s office with the paper carefully folded up to display the breaking story for *Bachelor Born*.

"This fellow you hired, Mr. Greneker. Look at this article. He's some kind of a genius. And this is his first day on the job. He's a find," said Sam with a straight face.

Sam was born and raised in the Bronx, where his family's home was not far from a pioneer silent film studio, The Gold Metal Studios on East 175th Street. He was a lean, tall, quick moving young man. If he had an opinion on any subject he liked to try it out on his colleagues. Once he made up his mind that he was right, he allowed no interference from Mayor LaGuardia on down. In fact, he welcomed encounters and felt invigorated by them.

If Sam was your friend, you had one for life. But, God help you if you betrayed a confidence. I recall a feud that ran for years with a trade paper editor. Sam had told the editor something in confidence and the editor made the mistake of telling Sam's producer. Judas Iscariot was never so harried from that day on as was that editor. Sam never let him forget it. And it didn't matter if the person was an editor of a daily, or head of a radio or TV program. In fact, I always suspected the higher placed the alleged wrongdoer, the more Sam relished letting him have it.

Harvey Sabinson, in his book, *Darling, You're Wonderful* tells of his experience as a college student when he was one of Sam's associate press agents. They were working the musical *Finian's Rainbow* which his brother, Lee Sabinson was producing.

Harvey made the mistake of requesting the afternoon off to attend his college graduation." Not on your life. Just because you are the producer's brother, don't think you deserve any special privileges around here. You'll stay here and paste up the scrapbook or you'll be fired. And I'll tell your brother Lee why," shrieked Sam.

Sound cruel? Oddly enough he could grin at his own manias, and did. It was hard to stay mad at Sam Friedman.

In his last years Sam waged just as valiant a battle against death as he waged on behalf of his clients. He was on a kidney dialysis machine for more than three years. At least he heard what his memorial service would have sounded like if there had been one. I, and some of his pals, tossed a luncheon party for Sam upstairs at Sardi's in the Belasco Room where we all swapped "Sam stories" and laughed till our sides ached.

Best of all, in his last 15 years, he was married to a young widow, Florence. Her daughter, Jayne, was as adoring of her step-dad as any child I have ever known. Jayne was also in show business, was one of the top public relation specialists in the pop-rock music field and was responsible for the international coverage of Woodstock.

I got infected by Sam's enthusiasm for stunts. The two of us arranged, by way of photographs, to have the unmarried male in the show that I was working on "engaged" to Jayne Manners, a statuesque blonde in Sam's show. Neither actor was privy to their "engagement."

We could not have chosen a more unlikely pair or one with such dire consequences to ourselves. Jayne, we learned to our chagrin, was J.J. Shubert's favorite mistress at the time. His ire at his own press department's attempt at match-making did not go unnoticed. Our boss, C.P. Greneker, was summoned on high to answer for it. Fortunately, C.P. handled it with aplomb and the subject was dropped.

I should have known better. I was well aware of J.J.'s shenanigans. I had seen him in action once too often. He was a womanizer and philanderer and took terrible advantage of his captive staff who he well knew had to succumb to his insatiable habits or be fired. This was in the middle of the Great Depression and jobs were hard to come by.

One day, "Grennie" called me into his office and asked that I go around to the various famous East Side New York hotels such as the Plaza, the Vanderbilt, the Ambassador, and others and snitch stationery and envelopes from their writing tables. Although I thoroughly disapprove of this kind of publicity I, as an associate press agent working for C.P. Greneker head of the Shuberts' publicity department, did what a good employee was told to do. When I returned with my "purloined letters," he then had his secretaries write flattering testimonials and send them off to various unsuspecting editors. Allegedly, they were from out-of- town visitors, always women, and they extolled the virtues of the productions they had seen. Of course, all were Shubert productions or those housed in Shubert-owned theatres. The letters frequently were printed.

Today's newspapers always check out the authenticity of the correspondent but, in those innocent times, many a bogus name and letter landed in the columns of some of the most august journals. Credit P.T. Barnum who coined the phrase, "There is a sucker born every minute."

As an associate press agent my working day was full. Copy had to be prepared for shows trying–out on tour, and others coming into New York. In those pre-TV days we spent a lot of time at our typewriters releasing information to the newspapers about our show as to the who, the what, and the where and the how, making sure full casts' names and schedules were correct.

In the 30's and 40's posters and broadsides were the norm for getting your story in front of the public. The two sign practitioners that I used for the Manhattan area were Jake and George Moxley. They would put up their wares anywhere and, it had been said, they were bold enough to put a sign on a baby carriage.

Jake was a believer in using his own two feet. He walked around town with window cards tucked under his arm. Rather cross-eyed, he'd squint his way up and down from 40$^{th}$ Street to 49$^{th}$ Street, plopping his cards in the various ticket agencies' windows, sometimes upside down. He smoked the foulest smelling cigars and probably the cheapest and could be sniffed yards before he arrived. A dead stump of his cigar, which he continually chewed, was just as devastating as the one fired up. To top it off, when he spoke in his Brooklyn accent his false teeth clicked. He had no trouble placing his window cards, for everyone said "Sure," just to get him downwind as quickly as they could.

Jake was proudest of his work for "The The-a-ter Guild," then in its zenith. Nights he would not be seen; but, come the dawn, you could spot his signs, all carefully stamped with his union's label, which frequently marred the artwork of the design, plastered on lampposts and newsstands.

His brother, George Moxley, was a different sort. He worked weekdays in New York and weekends in Red Bank, New Jersey, where he was a valued member of the Elks Club and a volunteer fireman. On weekends he made his living painting steeples. George was a barrel-chested, rolling-gait guy who wore loose fitting overalls. He drove an open-air half-ton truck that carried the paraphernalia of his trade; pots of glue, the signs he would put up and brushes in wild disarray. Cops knew and liked George and would protect his truck while he went into West Side office buildings to present his bills to the press agents. We all liked to engage him in conversation for, as a young Texan, he had run off to join the circus and had wonderful stories about the days he traveled with the "Savage Shows" and had to "skinny" up and down poles. We figured that's where he got his agility to climb those steeples.

On weekdays, he and his wife lived in a cold-water flat on 9$^{th}$ Avenue over a store. If you needed his services, you contacted him by night; during the day he was working at his trade.

The Moxley Brothers presented their handwritten bills to us and we would send them to the ad agency to be included as part of the agency's weekly advertising bill. It was the norm that many of the suppliers would have to wait more than a month to get paid. We considered that unfair when it came to the Moxleys and urged immediate payment.

The large billboard signs, consisting of 24 separate sheets pasted together, were handled by a father and son team, John Moran and John Jr., and they would often put their sheets on any flat surface they could find. I could always tell when the Morans did a particularly good job by the anguished calls from a property owner who had tracked down our press department by calling the box-office of the show we were publicizing.

"Some bastard, in the night, has put up a poster for your show on my store wall facing Queens Boulevard. If it isn't down by tomorrow, I'll sue,"

Our answer was always the same; "We'll see to it that it is taken down right away, Sir (or Madam), but, in the meantime would you like to see our show? We'll be glad to arrange gratis tickets for you and your spouse any night but Friday or Saturday." Usually, free tickets did the trick and we were able to keep the Moran billboard up.

After John Senior died, the billboard business died with him and in its place were large, illuminated, outdoor advertising signs. These displays were contracted directly by our ad agency but, as associate press agents, it was our job to inspect these posters in the five boroughs. This required that we ride around in the outdoor advertising company's limousine, to make sure the signs were indeed up and current. It was a pretty nice way to spend the day. It also included a free meal at one of the better restaurants such as Brooklyn's Gage and Tollner. It was a day away from the phones and the grind, and instructive to an out–of–towner like me. I learned about the history of the various sections of New York, the people who inhabited them, and their traffic patterns.

All this, plus setting up interviews and arranging photo sessions filled a good six-day week. Employees were expected to be on hand weekday nights and sometimes for Saturday matinees.

Curtain time was at 8:30, with casts reporting in half an hour early. If I left my office at 5:00, it gave me enough time to hop on the subway and head out to our apartment in Kew Gardens, in Washington Heights, for an early dinner with Bobbie and our infant daughter, Judy, and get back to town in time to catch the evening performance. It was the only time except Sundays we had family time together other than Wednesday evenings. I was too stage struck to mind the awful hours and kept meeting myself coming and going on the subway.

As I settled into my seat on the subway before rush hour I began to think about my new job as an associate publicist for the Shubert Organization and of my young family who were living in Kew Gardens. How lucky I was to be working in New York City at something I really loved and to have Bobbie and Judy just a half hour away from downtown New York on the E or F train. The town had been established in the late 19<sup>th</sup> century and was named Kew Gardens after the famous botanical gardens in England. This was a lawn and tree community, quite a contrast to the cement sidewalks of New York.

It was Wednesday and I had already checked the matinees at the Morosco and Majestic Theaters and dug up some items to send to the papers the next day. This being Wednesday, with two performances, it meant that I could fade away at 5:00 and I would not have to come back in to check the night's show. I considered that one of the perks of my job.

I carried the evening papers with me, The *Tribune* and The *Times* which I would peruse and Bobbie would also enjoy. I would be home tonight to help Bobbie feed and bathe baby Judy, who would turn two years old next month.

Daydreaming, I thought about our past summer in Whitefield. It had been a magical summer in New Hampshire with our cabin facing the Presidential Range of the White Mountains. I had been asked to come back this summer and I yearned to do so, but I knew in my heart of hearts, that, with the responsibility of a family, I needed a job that would produce more revenue this summer than did the one in New Hampshire. My job with the Shuberts was giving me an adequate income but Broadway closed down in the summers due to the excessive heat; air-conditioning hadn't been introduced.

I had been offered a summer job with Irving Hoffman, a cartoonist turned press agent for a little more money than Whitefield. I could learn a lot from him particularly how to write for columnists. Hoffman had a direct pipeline to Walter Winchell. Irving also worked for a lot of film companies and those personal contacts might be invaluable. Should I jump ship?

Jackson Heights stop already? I better get myself ready to leap up and jump off this subway; the Kew Garden's stop was approaching rapidly.

It was a short walk across the park to our furnished flat. I never worried that the apartment wasn't grander. I thought that Bobbie was a good sport to put up with it. I also appreciated her willingness to make the transition from Philadelphia to New York with me. Perhaps it helped that her half-sister, Janet, lived not too far away in Freeport, Long Island. I was lucky to have such a wonderful wife.

One of my earliest chores, working for the Shuberts, was to travel up to Columbus Circle to the Wall Street Journal's uptown office and inform Mr. Smith, the then theater editor, that unless he printed our releases and photos from the Shubert ménage with more regularity, Mr. Hearst himself would be informed and dire consequences of a commercial nature might follow. I could not have been very convincing and why Greenie thought a neophyte was better to brave this sanctum than a seasoned publicist beats me. But, I was treated with courtesy, chiefly I suspect, because C.P. was such a liberal dispenser of passes to all the Hearst employees. One secretary, Eileen Eagan, had, it seemed to me only one function; to relay these daily pass requests along to the press agents.

I learned early that the longevity of a show on Broadway was directly related to the number of seats filled per performance. A not-so-magical formula was used that simply indicated when a theater would begin to lose money because of empty seats. At that point the play closed and the publicist looked for another job. There is one exception to the rule however; if you own the theater and if you are the producer of the play, then any options are open to you.

Mr. J.J. was often in Budapest, Vienna or Berlin, scouting for operettas, his first love. He found the Strausses to be goldmines with one exception and that would be the one Strauss play to which I was assigned. *The Three Waltzes*, starring the lovely Kitty Carlisle as Marie Hiller, opened in the Shubert's Majestic Theater on December 25th, 1937.

Kitty, a vision of beauty and an auditory delight, was just beginning her acting career. She was two years my senior and we would grow up in the theater together, working at the Bucks County Playhouse where she met her husband-to-be, Moss Hart, and then in New Hope, where we would both reside. In later years Kitty would take a real interest in promoting the arts and would become head of New York State's Arts Council.

*The Three Waltzes* had been a hit in Paris and London starring Yvonne Printemps and Sasha Guitry, but on this side of the Atlantic it was nothing more than big and boring. Opulent yes, box-office, no. If it had been in any other theater, it would have closed but not in J.J. Shubert's Majestic Theater. He just loved all those waltzes and the lovely women in their gorgeous gowns, swishing around the dance floor.

So, if the show crept above the stop-clause, that elusive figure that determined whether a show could be given notice to vacate, it really didn't matter. J.J. kept it running for 122 performances.

J.J also forced more revenue by sending his shows on the road (to the Shubert theaters, of course). This system engendered the illegal monopoly litigation in the 1950's. The Shuberts were convicted on a monopoly charge in violation of the Sherman and Clayton anti-trust acts. They "sold" the road shows and even extended their New York runs with phony publicity, quotations and doctored reviews and just outright lies in the newspapers telling the public how good the shows were and how popular they were.

My two years'education with the Shubert Organization taught me what not to do, as a press agent. Perhaps that in itself was a good learning experience. As I matured in my work as a press agent, I found that the relationship between agent and The Press had to be one of complete trust; my information and articles had to speak the truth. Editors counted on agents for accurate information and once that trust was broken, they would never let you forget it.

*Scene 3*

## Bucks County Playhouse

The 23-year-old New York actor, St John Terrell, nicknamed Sinjin (that is how the name St John is pronounced in England), hired me in the summer of 1939 to be his press agent for the Bucks County Playhouse in New Hope, PA. It happened that Bobbie was familiar with the Bucks County area and thought the experience would be a good one for both of us. She also believed that Judy, age three, would enjoy a summer in the country. Little did we know then that our one summer's stay in Bucks County would extend for another 51 years.

Sinjin, although he was more like a snake oil salesmen than an actor/promoter, did help the New Hope community establish a summer theater on the banks of the Delaware by restoring the Old Hope Mill. My daughter Babs remembers him as a scary fire-eater at the local festivals. Thus The Bucks County Playhouse was born on July 1, 1939. Sinjin, who demanded too much of management during the course of his short-lived contract, was fired within the year by the Board. I always felt, and still do, that Sinjin was not treated fairly by the Board and was dismissed for little reason. At any rate, he continued his scheming and promoting, moved to Lambertville, NJ and in 1949, successfully established the tented Lambertville Music Circus which was in direct competition with the Bucks County Play House although their playbills were very different from each other.

The opening night was spectacular, and *Springtime for Henry* by Edward Everett Horton was well received with Mr. Horton himself playing the lead. My publicity for the event worked wonders. The 300 seats were not only filled but there were 50 standees (that practice of letting people stand in the back of the theater would soon to be illegal because of the fire marshal laws in both PA and NJ). We had a star studded audience; George S. Kaufman, Moss Hart, Burgess Meredith, Orson Welles, Florence McGree, Jack Kirkland, Haila Stoddard, Kenyon Nickolson and George Spelvin to name just a few.

On opening night Richard Bennett, the matinee idol of the stage and early silent movie era, stood up in one of the small balcony areas boxes on the left hand side of the theater, and gave too long an introduction. He obviously had been drinking too much and flubbed his final remarks. As he droned on he finally announced with great bravado: "This place will become a hallowed spot to which, each summer, pilgrims of Thespis will wend their way.

No longer will Austria hold monopoly on theatrical shrines! Yes, friends, we'll do it! We'll make New Hope the Stroudsburg of America." Of course, what he meant was Salzburg, not Stroudsburg. After he sat down, a friend pointed out to him his faux pas. Then, to add insult to injury, he interrupted the play to correct himself.

During the preparations for our theater opening, the board arranged to have Charles Child, a young local painter, paint scenes of New Hope on the stage curtain of the Bucks County Playhouse. It was a beautiful rendition and quite avant garde.

As fortune would have it, *Look Magazine*, in its late spring edition liked the idea of the painted curtain, along with my article describing the new summer theater in New Hope, and gave us an unbelievable double spread in the magazine. What a coup for a kid of 27, who was just beginning his career as a press agent.

Besides being a painter of note, Charles had a twin brother, Paul. As identical twins, Charles and Paul enjoyed fooling friends as to their true identity. In 1946, Paul married Julia who became the famous Culinary Queen, Julia Child. I often wondered whether Julia had trouble telling the boys apart.

I was quite proud of the double spread in *Look,* but the sketch of opening night by Al Hirschfeld, printed in the Sunday Drama section of the *New York Times* was true magic and a triumph for any press agent. And how did all this happen?

*Al Hirschfeld's rendering of the opening of the
Bucks County Playhouse, July 1ˢᵗ, 1939*

*From left to right: Moss Hart, Beatrice Kaufman,
George S. Kaufman and Richard Bennett*

I had convinced my friend, Lewis Nichols, who, in 1939 was drama editor for the *New York Times* and who later became drama critic following Brooks Atkinson's retirement, that the opening of the Bucks Country Playhouse in New Hope would make good copy for his Sunday drama section. He liked the idea and assigned Al Hirschfeld to do one of his signature sketches of opening night. The Hirschfeld drawing, along with an article, resulted in an eight-column spread in the Sunday *Times* drama section. It was an unheard-of achievement. Look closely at the drawing and you can see Sinjin Terrell on the run, along with Moss Hart, Beatrice Kaufman, George S. Kaufman, and Richard Bennett. It was an impressive group for opening night.

Because Sinjin was being replaced, the Board of Trustees needed someone who could manage and direct the Playhouse. Margaret Lynley, a casting director living in Bucks County, suggested her friends, Theron and Phyllis Bamberger. After receiving a positive nod from the Board, she convinced the Bambergers to come to New Hope to take a look and to get a feel for the place. Theron seemed interested enough to apply to Sinjun for my job as press agent but, thank goodness, was turned down. Fortunately, Sinjin told him, "I already have a press agent, Sol Jacobson, and I am very well satisfied with him." Theron Bamberger took the job of producer and in the years that followed parlayed the Bucks County Theater into one of the finest summer theaters in the country. Theron even hired me for a second summer as press agent but it would be my last. By the summer of 1941 my schedule was full and, at the end of the summer, I would be heading to New York to work with Theron's wife, Phyllis, as an associate press agent in the George Abbott organization.

But before I left New Hope, Theron gave me some good pointers and sound advice as to how to best "cover" each Broadway performance when I got to the big city.

"When you get to the theater, stop in front of the box-office, say hello to the company manager, who, unless he has been held up, will have no news for you. Then go through the pass door from the auditorium to the backstage. Say 'Hi' to the stage manager, knock on the star's dressing room door and wish her well, ditto to her leading man. Then get the hell out through the stage door and go see another show or go home."

Was that Bamberger a cynic or a realist or maybe some of each? With his own productions I warrant he required more of his press agents, but I found that a daily visit was a must. Matinee days, Wednesdays and Saturdays there were two performances. I usually covered the matinees on those days which meant I could be home with my wife and young daughter on Wednesday and Saturday nights.

An awfully funny incident happened during my second summer. During the summer months, when temperatures rise to uncomfortable degrees, the local kids enjoy a cool swim in Ingham Springs and Creek. It happens to be the most productive spring in Southeastern Pennsylvania which guarantees that there is always plenty of water in which to swim.

When casting the play, *Boy Meets Girl,* Sinjin looked desperately for a British-type to play the small part of the distinguished representative of an overseas film company. He found such a person in his elderly Stage Manager, Dennis Gurney. Dennis was perfect for the part; he was English and looked smashing in an English Derby hat.

Dennis was thrilled to be included and decided, in celebration of his new role as an actor, that he would go for a swim with the kids in the cool, clear waters of Ingham Creek. He dove off the dam into the pool, swimming about, showing off with the vigor of a much younger man, much to the delight of the other swimmers. However, all was short-lived, for Dennis, after some fancy underwater swimming, came to the surface gasping for air. The huffing and puffing that ensued was too much for his set of "uppers" and the dentures shot from his mouth to disappear into the depths of the Creek. What to do? Dennis was supposed to go on stage in hours and he could hardly sound like a distinguished Englishman with his upper-plate missing.

The news of the accident spread like wild fire and, within an hour, the whole town was looking for Dennis Gurney's "uppers." A new fangled device was summoned that obviously had been used before to find missing articles. The underwater contraption looked like an old-hot water tank with windows; hoses came out of the top, hooked to a bicycle pump which allowed the participant to breathe. A young volunteer got in and submerged and believe it or not, within a short time, surfaced with a set of "uppers." The country was saved! Dennis had already gone to the Playhouse to prepare for his stage entrance but was none too happy with the prospects of babbling his lines due to his lack of teeth.

Just in time, our hero, the young volunteer, with denture in hand, ran through the stage door into the theater where he found Dennis about to go on stage. Grabbing the "uppers" from him, Dennis slammed the teeth inside his mouth and walked on stage to begin his role.

Ah, but it was not to be. Within seconds, an irate woman came running into the theater, with a noisy little dog, demanding, "Where's that man? Where's that man?"

"Sh-h-h-h, please" whispered Sinjin. "What Man?"

"Well, that man" exclaimed the woman, pointing to Dennis on stage. "He's got my teeth, he's got my teeth."

A trip with the woman backstage didn't quiet her in the least. She was still demanding that Dennis had her teeth, as Dennis made his exit from the stage.

As Dennis emerged from the stage, he was not a happy camper. "Something happened to my teeth as they lay in the Creek," Dennis announced. "For some reason they don't fit properly." Just one look at his mouth and it was obvious; these were not

Dennis' uppers. "Give me my teeth" screamed the lady with the nasty little dog.

Getting them out of Dennis' mouth was a problem. Because he had used such force to seat them, there was no way they could be dislodged from his mouth. Everybody tried; Sinjin, the stage hands, the make-up women and even the costume mistress, all to no avail. Finally, Dennis was placed stomach down on the top of the stairs with his head dangling. Sinjin, from below, with his fingers grasping Dennis' recalcitrant uppers and with the rest of the stage hands holding on to one another down the stairs, started pulling; one, two, three, and out they came as the stage hands fell, cascading down the stairs.

The woman with the nasty dog picked up her dentures, inspected to see if they were in one piece, wiped them off, plopped them into her mouth and was off, never to be seen again.

We never did find Dennis's!

While I was working at the Bucks County Playhouse we rented an apartment garage on Rabbit Run Road from a singing teacher. The word singing was an anomaly, for the teacher could not sing nor could her students and her lack of tonal quality was the impetus that made Bobbie look seriously for a house in the neighborhood. We both got to a point where we could not take the teacher's screeching and screaming any more.

Bobbie was familiar with the area. As a teenager she had been to New Hope many times; barge parties and outings sponsored by the Christian Science Church.

Bobbie started looking in earnest for a place the Jacobson's could call their own. A number of prerequisites fell into the equation. The house had to be near enough New Hope so the family could walk to town. The second; someplace not of the norm. It had to be different and perhaps modern. When Bobbie was at Bennington College one of the visiting professors was Frank Lloyd Wright, the famous architect. At one of his lectures, Wright deplored the architecture at Bennington, saying the planner missed an opportunity by designing very traditional buildings rather than going for something more modern. Bobbie took this to heart while looking for a house. She was looking for something different.

On Windy Bush Road, within two miles of New Hope, we found what we were looking for. Inez McCombs, a painter by trade was the current owner. The house was far from a traditional dwelling. Ultra modern, especially for 1939, it had both charm and warmth and it sat on a double lot which would give us protection from our neighbors, at least on one side. A few problems; the windows reminded us of factory windows and didn't open too well, and the whole house was painted black.

We settled on the house quickly and my father was good enough to put up the $ 10,000 to seal the deal. We, both in our late twenties, were hardly financially capable of such expenditure and were very thankful that Grandpa came to the rescue.

One of our first chores was repainting the house white, killing that deadly black look. In the fifty seven plus years of ownership we made many changes to the inside and outside, one of which was to put a full bedroom and bath on the first floor. It was here that my mother-in-law, Jessalyn Scott, stayed during the spring and summer months when she wasn't in residence with her other daughter, Janet. And, oh yes, we built a delightful pond in the backyard where the girls spent many hours watching the frogs and goldfish among the water lilies.

As the years rolled by there were many individuals who graced our Windy Bush Road home. Among the most notable were Theron and Phyllis Bamberger who ran the Bucks County Play House for ten years.

The Spewaks, Bella and Samuel, were good friends and they wrote the book to *Kiss Me Kate.* The show opened on Broadway in *1948* with music and lyrics by Cole Porter.

Mira Nakashima was the daughter of George Nakashima, furniture designer and father of the American craft movement. They lived around the corner from us and at the age of five, Mira was Babs' first friend.

I didn't learn of this story until my discharge from the Army, but it still fascinates me:

George Nakashima, a US citizen, a graduate architect plus a master's degree from MIT, was interned in the "War Relocation Camps" because of his Japanese ancestry. Fortunately, a fellow architect, Antonin Raymond had him released and George settled New Hope.

While I was in the service, my father, hearing of George's plight and realizing the family was hard-pressed, commissioned him to design a desk for my daughter, Judy. My wife, Bobbie, thrilled with the design, wished to share it with me and sent the drawings to where I was stationed in Europe. The only problem; I never got them. And so, floating round somewhere in Europe, in someone's old trunk, is an invaluable Nakashima design of a child's desk.

Actress Blythe Danner, who feels the Jacobsons "changed her life," was a frequent visitor.

## *My Nine months with George Abbott*

It was Phyllis Perlman, press agent for the icon, George Abbott, who suggested I work with her as an associate press agent in George Abbott's office.

Always at the ready to advance my career, I accepted and began working for this remarkable showman in the fall of 1939. One of the first shows I worked on was *See My Lawyer* which opened in September of that year. One of my chores was escorting Milton Berle, the star, to the radio studio for an interview. I am still waiting for that 50 cents he owes me.

The play was not a booming success and closed in April of 1940, but I met and worked with two men who became close friends of mine, Bobby Griffith, the stage manager for the show who later became a director with Hal Prince, and Carl Fisher, Abbott's nephew, the business manager. Once again, although I didn't know it at the time, both of these men would play a vital role in my career as a press agent.

I found Abbott to be a wonderful, professional man, an admirable producer, a remarkable playwright, a director who was absolutely indomitable in victory or defeat. It didn't matter whether the show was a success or failure; his expression was always the same. He'd take it in and then say, "What's the next project?"

There was no monkey business with George Abbott. The day after a show opened he would hold a meeting to discuss the previous night's performance and then talk about the next show he was opening. And that was typical of a George Abbott production; keep moving and don't let any grass grow under your feet. "You know, don't look back. What's the next show?" George Abbott had a most professional attitude toward the theater.

George also had a fetish when it came to a clean desk. It had to be spotless and clear which meant a lot a material landed in the waste basket. One day this clean desk idea backfired and he inadvertently threw away some US War Bonds that he had purchased. The staff had to go through all the trash bins in the basement to find the missing bonds.

George liked to foster the notion that he was a skinflint, because he didn't like to pay high salaries during the depression. But I don't believe he actually cared that much about dough; he wasn't what we call "money mad." Although I never went along because I preferred to spend Thanksgiving dinner with my family, George, the big spender, would take the company to the Automat on Thanksgiving for lunch between the matinee and evening performances.

As Phyllis's associate, my duty was to get out a release a day for the Abbott shows that were running. There were eight papers that needed copy, the most important for us in show business being *The Brooklyn Eagle* and the *Bronx Home News*. Keeping the editors of these papers with proper copy kept me very busy. My job was also to cover the shows at least four nights a week plus Saturday which gave me plenty of ammunition for my releases to the paper.

In the nine months while with Phyllis I worked on six plays, *Too Many Girls* being the most noteworthy.This musical comedy was produced by George Abbott with music by Richard Rodgers, lyrics by Lorenz Hart and book by George Marion Jr. It opened at the Imperial Theater on October 18, 1939 and ran for 239 performances on Broadway. It later went on the road and then RKO films showed interest and *Too Many Girls* became a movie.

The New York Times claimed the Broadway show an instant hit saying "Sets you swaying to some of the most enchanting music the gifted Rodgers has ever written, matched by some of Mr. Hart's most felicitous and audacious lyrics." The song, "I Didn't Know What Time It Was" sticks out in my mind and I can still sing the lyrics.

Perhaps of most interest were the men in the cast, all my contemporaries in age, who later became stars.

While vacationing in Florida, Lorenz Hart heard a young man who was leading a small combo band in a night club in Miami. He was taken by the young man's talent and he convinced the youngster to come to New York, promising him a spot in one of the New York clubs. The young man had been born in Santiago de Cuba and was named Desiderio Alberto Arnaz y de Acha III. Once in New York he shortened his name to Desi Arnaz. While casting *Too Many Girls*, Hart suggested Desi be given one of the parts, that of a football player from Argentina. Knowing that Desi had no acting experience, Hart coached him for his audition. Desi got the part and became a sensation over night.

Following the play's closing, Desi went to Hollywood where he performed in the movie version of *Too Many Girls.* It was in Hollywood that he met and married the comedian Lucille Ball and, in the early 50s the TV show *I love Lucy* was born which became an immediate hit. Desi played Ricky Ricardo, a Cuban band leader and Lucy's husband.

In addition to Desi Arnaz, the handsome Van Johnson appeared as a dancer in the chorus line. He was to become a major film star at Metro-Goldwyn-Mayer during and after WWII.

The third young man of note was Eddie Bracken, not a new-comer to the stage, performing in vaudeville at the age of nine. But it was in our show, playing the part of Jo Jo Jordon where his comedy acting career gained fame. A movie career followed thanks to Hollywood director Preston Sturges who cast Bracken in two of Sturges best loved films,

*Hail to the Conquering Hero* and *The Miracle of Morgan Creek* with Betty Hutton as his leading lady. Due to the popularity of these films and "The Eddie Bracken Show" on radio, Eddie's name became a household word during the War years.

*Young Judy and my wife Bobbie after a cool swim*

In the summer of 1940 I returned to New Hope as the press agent for The Buck's County Play House, hired this time by Theron Bamberger, Phyllis's husband. With our residence now in New Hope working locally for the summer gave me much needed time with my wife and daughter, four year old Judy.

In the early Fall of 1940 another career change. I became one of Richard S. Maney's "China Boys."

*Scene* **5**

*Arsenic*

In the early fall of 1940, Richard S. Maney had just released one of his associates who was spending too much time worrying about the ups and downs of the stock market and not paying enough attention to being a conscientious press agent. I was lucky enough to fill that vacancy.

My first assignment was in Baltimore where a new show called *Arsenic and Old Lace* was opening.

Joseph Kesselring, who lived in a boarding house in North Newtown, Kansas, taught English at Bethel College. He wrote 12 plays but only one was successful, and even that one would have fallen by the wayside if it were not for the efforts of Howard Lindsay, a theatrical producer, playwright, librettist, director and actor and his partner, Russell (Buck) Crouse, a playwright and librettist.

The Lindsay and Crouse partnership, which lasted a lifetime, began in 1934 when they revised the P.G Wodehouse/Guy Bolton book for Cole Porter's very successful musical *Anything Goes.*

Perhaps the partners' best known work was their adaptation into a Broadway play of Clarence Day Jr.'s stories about his father, Clarence Day Sr., which were printed in article form in the *New Yorker Magazine* in 1936. The re-write became *Life with Father,* which made its debut on Broadway in 1939 and ran for seven years, a record run. Howard Lindsay played the lead as the Father and his wife, Dorothy Stickney, played opposite him as the Mother.

In order to get their plays purchased, authors' agents would send copies of their works to various members of the theatrical community. That's how Dorothy Stickney came upon Joseph Kesselring's play, *Bodies in the Basement.* At night, after coming home from the theater, she had a habit of reading the new plays that were sent to her husband, Howard. If she found something she liked perhaps some arrangement could be made with the author to produce his work. It was one way to help advance her husband's career.

As she read Kesselring's script, she was intrigued by the story-line, that of two elderly ladies who poisoned their male boarders and buried them in the basement. But the play was not funny enough and, as she finished her reading, she said to herself, "I'll bet the boys can rewrite this and make something out of it." The boys, her husband,

Howard and his partner, Buck, agreed; they would re-write the play and produce it. Kesselring agreed but there was a stipulation: Joseph Kesselring was to be listed as the sole author. The only mention of Lindsay or Crouse was as producers. So insistent was the author about these stipulations that a special note was printed on the "All rights Reserved" page:

> Anyone receiving permission to produce ARSENIC AND OLD LACE is required to give credit to the Author as sole and exclusive Author of the Play on the title page of all programs distributed in connection with performances of the Play and in all instances in which the title of the Play appears for purposes of advertising, publicizing or otherwise exploiting the Play and/or a production thereof. The name of the Author must appear on a separate line, in which no other name appears, immediately beneath the title and in size of type equal to 50% of the size of the largest, most prominent letter used for the title of the Play. No person, firm or entity may receive credit larger or more prominent than that accorded to the Author.

On the 10th of January, 1941, *Arsenic and Old Lace* by Joseph Kesselring opened in the Fulton Theater in New York after less than a four week trial run in Baltimore. Later that year it moved to the newly rehabilitated Hudson Theater which Lindsay and Crouse had purchased, on west 44th street.

Dick Maney loathed going out of town. So, as one of Maney's associates I was assigned as press agent for *Arsenic and Old Lace* during its initial tryout run in Baltimore at Ford's Theater. As I look back on my many years of working with Maney, this assignment, that of helping to get *Arsenic and Old Lace* on the road, was the one I enjoyed most. It was also where I had a chance to meet the stars of the show, Josephine Hull, and Boris Karloff who played a supporting role. I found both of them to be engaging, especially Boris, who in my mind had always been a "monster."

Boris was delighted to finally make it to Broadway. He had been in movies as the monster in *Frankenstein*, and he was looking for a change of venue. Certainly as Jonathan, Aunt Abby's nephew, he had that opportunity.

Boris was born William Henry Pratt and was always considered the black sheep of the family; he stuttered badly and had a lisp. As a youth he was so determined to get into show business that he ran away from home. It was in Hollywood that he changed his name to Boris Karloff. The stuttering he overcame but, if you look at his early *Frankenstein* movies, you will notice that he continued to lisp, an impediment that lasted his whole stage and screen career. I found Boris not to be a monster at all, but a very warm individual.

During the trial run of a play, changes in the script are common. If ever a comedy was rewritten by phone it was *Arsenic*. Russell Crouse (Buck) and Bretaigne Windust (Windy) were on the phone in Baltimore while Howard Lindsay and Anna Erskine, later to become Mrs. Crouse, were on the other end of the line, in the Empire Offices in New York.

I remember one day going to Baltimore with a big fat envelope of re-writes and delivering it to director Windust. The re-writes were hot from the typewriter of Lindsay and Crouse. Buck had been in Baltimore watching it with audiences but had come back to New York to polish the script with his partners, Howard and Erskine.

We were pressed for time because Howard and Buck insisted that *Arsenic* hit New York City before *Mr. and Mrs. North,* another new comedy scheduled for Broadway.

So, our run in Baltimore was cut short a few days to achieve that supposed advantage. However, we were able to squeeze an extra performance in by raising the curtain on Sunday night to a specially invited audience, something that was verboten in those days.

The opening night of *Arsenic* was like launching a rocket and it blasted off far beyond our expectations. I'm sure Crouse was numb because after the opening he couldn't help but ask *Variety's* drama critic, Hobe Morrison, if he thought it had a chance.

"Have a chance," replied Hobe. "You'll make a fortune, you chump."

The next day, the line of theater-goers was unbroken from the Fulton Street Theater, now the Helen Hayes Theater, all the way down to Broadway. This was early 1941. I went away to war in 1943 and stayed overseas for 14 months and after I came home, *Arsenic* was still playing to delighted audiences. It had become the darling of West End audiences in wartime London, and even hit the road with Erich Van Stroheim in the U.S.

Even today, in the twenty first century, *Arsenic and Old Lace* is one of the favorite dramatic works, playing in high schools and repertory theaters throughout the country.

On opening night in New York, I was leaning against the wall on the side of the theater with my eyes glued on Brooks Atkinson; I was interested in seeing his reaction to a particular scene in the middle of Act 1.

One of the prerequisites of being a drama critic is to show as little emotion as possible while in the theater. Critics don't like to tip their hand before typing their columns. Actually, Brooks never typed his columns; he wrote them all out in long hand, leaving the typing to others.

It was during this scene in *Arsenic and Old Lace* that Brooks let it all out.

The scene, paraphrased: Nephew Mortimer has just told his Aunt Abby that he and Elaine are going to be married. Excited, Aunt Abby tells her sister the good news. Aunt Martha has just entered from the kitchen, and both put their arms around Mortimer to congratulate him. Mortimer is distracted. He pulls back the window curtain and looks out. He is staring at a bird perched on a statue. His Aunt is curious as to what he sees. He points to the statue and indicates he's looking at a red crested swallow which he calls by it's Latin name, Horundinada Cornina (a made up word). "No," Aunt Martha retorts, "that is the statue of Emma B.

Stout." "No, says Mortimer, not the statue, but the bird sitting on it. I've only seen that bird once before."

Atkinson, who up to this scene was in his usual critic pose, arms across his chest, flailed his arms in the air and broke into hysterics. Brooks Atkinson never laughs in the theater; he is a most reserved individual. Well, he gave up that night. He just roared; he held his sides, unable to contain himself.

I was pleased to see that he got it. He figured out, as I already knew, that Lindsay and Crouse had written that scene for him. He was an avid bird-watcher and had even taken me on one of his bird walks.

Brooks could interest his readers with his appreciation better than any journalist before or since and his columns were required reading by anyone interested in the theater.

Dick Maney taught me a lot when it came to creative publicity. With *Arsenic* he publicized the men and women who backed the production. They were a distinguished lot: many of them were writers, such as Mrs. Margaret Cullman, Frank Sullivan, the Saratoga based retired humor columnist and a *New Yorker* contributor, and Maney himself. Whenever Dick could cajole them into it, he'd get a piece about some fancied slight of the injured stockholder attacking Lindsay and Crouse. It made good, if arcane, copy. My favorite was a Frank Sullivan column protesting Crouse's inability to look like a prosperous producer with those baggy suits that always gave the impression he slept in them. The headline appeared on the usually unimaginative *Sun's* page:

"Crouse's Wrinkles Wrankle." I suspect Maney wrote that headline.

An interesting aside: the living room setting of *Arsenic and Old Lace,* where the Brewster sisters did their dirty work, resembled the living room of the boarding house occupied by Joseph Kesselring during his tenure at Bethel College. It was called Goerz House in those days and is now the home of the college president.

*Scene* **6**

## The King of Press Agents, Richard Sylvester Maney

Dick Maney refused to leave New York no matter who requested his services.

As his associate, I was answering the phone one day when a man with a British accent called and asked to speak to his good friend, Dick. To my question "Who shall I say is calling," the surprising answer was, "Charlie Chaplin."

Dick later told me, that when he was a student at the University of Washington in Seattle, he had worked as an usher at the Empress Theater. One of the acts that had played was Fred Karno's London Company with their four "Karno's Klowns." One of the "Klowns" was Charlie Chaplin. Dick and Charlie became life-long friends. After Chaplin joined the Keystone Studios and become famous, he asked his friend Dick if he would come to Los Angles to be his press agent. Dick, who referred to his friend as "Lotus Man," (those who eat the lotus blossom and have delusions) told him emphatically," No." He preferred to stay and work in New York.

Dick Maney was a well known New York press agent and a man for whom I had great admiration and respect. The article in *Time Magazine*, in January of 1940, "Portrait of a Press Agent" describes him well; "With his Irish mug and scarred nose, Maney—who in appearance is a roustabout George M. Cohan—looks the part he plays." Tough, but with a soft touch, he was everyone's friend. His publicity articles were so well written an editor had a hard time turning them down.

The first time I saw Dick Maney in New York was in 1937 when my career was just getting started in the Big Apple. I was sent by Greneker to deliver an article to Billy Rose in his penthouse suite atop a 42$^{nd}$ Street office building, between 6$^{th}$ and 7$^{th}$ Avenues. I was surprised when I saw Maney manning the switch- board. It was the old plug-in variety. All the help must have been out to lunch because Dick was putting calls through, alerting the press about one of Billy Rose's, "The "Little Maestro's," latest works. I was impressed that a man with Maney's stature and reputation as a press agent would be operating a switchboard. But it did tell me something about the man. Manual labor didn't bother him one bit if he wanted to get something done. He knew how to roll up his shirtsleeves.

Shortly after my seeing him as a switchboard operator, Dick moved his office down the street to The Empire Theater where he had a large room directly over the marquee. It was on Broadway facing the Metropolitan Opera House, one door away from 40th Street. It was here, in late 1940, that I started work as one of his associates. My desk was in one of the alcoves with a window. The ledge outside my window was large and filled with pigeons and their droppings. I often wondered if I couldn't start my own "Victory Garden" on the ledge; the droppings were certainly fertile enough.

There are all kinds of chores an advance man has to do but getting a referee for a cricket match was out of the ordinary.

It was 1941 and it was Dick who suggested to Guthrie McClintic's manager, Stanley Gilkey, that he hire me as the press agent for *Spring Again*, a play written by Isabel Leighton and Bertram Bloch. It opened in New York at The Henry Miller's Theater in November of '41, and then moved to the Playhouse Theater until the summer of '42. Its star-studded cast included Grace George and C. Aubrey Smith who were in their eighties at the time and, I am pleased to report, they never missed a performance and that means eight times a week. The play was a success and ran for 241 performances.

Because of its success, McClintic, who directed the play, decided to take it on the road along with yours truly. It was my first experience of being an "on the road" press agent. One of our stops was Chicago.

Lloyd Lewis was drama editor for The *Chicago Daily News* and a good friend. He was an Indiana Quaker who matriculated through Swarthmore College and, to his credit as a Lincoln authority, wrote a book of essays titled, *Myths After Lincoln*. While at Swarthmore he became fond of the game of cricket thanks to his friends at nearby Haverford College. He was so enamored with the sport that he set up a cricket league in his current home town of Evanston, Illinois. On Sunday next, the league was having a big game and needed a referee; would I be good enough to ask Sir C. Aubrey Smith if he would consider doing it. Lloyd was well aware that Smith, besides being a good English character actor, was also a star on the cricket field. He was a true cricketer and it was said that his oddly curved bowling run-up gave him the nickname "Round the Corner Smith." Sir Aubrey's answer to my question, "Be delighted to, old boy."

I was standing outside the theater while I was in Boston trying out *Spring Again,* and Josh Logan, a director with whom I had worked when I was with the Shubert organization, came to chat. We gabbed about a show called *Battle of Angels* which had not been well received and was about to close. "You know," he said to me, "the play is written by an unknown by the name of Tom Williams, but this is not the last time you will hear from this playwright."

It was during this time that our second child, Babs was born. I was home in New Hope for the birth but, according to my wife, I wasn't much help. Bobbie said that when she went into labor, I was seen reading a book, held upside down. When we were to leave for the Trenton hospital my wife insisted that she take the time to put on her garter belt so that her stockings would stay up. I was so nervous and she so slow that I finally said, "If you don't leave now, I am leaving without you."

The garter belt was attached and we did get to the hospital on time. Barbara (Babs) Jacobson entered this world on April 16th, 1942. Of course, she was a beautiful baby.

Dick Maney never interfered or tried to mastermind one of his associates' projects, but he would make helpful suggestions when necessary. While he never liked to hit the road himself, he was delighted to assign one of his associates as a "road man," that is if they cared to go out with the show. I enjoyed being a "roadman" getting out of town and meeting with various editors across the country.

In the late Fall of 1942, I found myself in Philadelphia. Maney had assigned me to Thornton Wilder's play *Skin of Our Teeth,* which would later win a Pulitzer Prize for Drama.

I was always grateful to go to Philadelphia because it meant an extra night or two at home in New Hope with Bobbie, my six year old Judy and baby Babs, instead of staying in a lonely second class hotel room in New York.

Tallulah Bankhead was one of the stars of *Skin of Our Teeth* with a number of understudies.

One of the understudies was a full-blown, bosomy beauty, with a deep throaty voice, whose talents one of the producers fancied in more ways than one. So too, it turned out, did one of the managers, a direct and breezy Broadway citizen.

On separate occasions I was summoned to their offices.

"Sol, you going to Philly next week ahead of the show?" inquired the producer.

"Yes sir. Anything I can do for you?"

"There is, but be discreet about it, please. Ask the manager of the Ritz Carlton to give the understudy a large suite, and see to it that my room adjoins and that it has an opening door to her suite."

"Will do."

A few days later, unbeknownst to the producer, I was summoned to the manager's office for the same request. The phrase, "be discreet" was once again emphasized.

Doing my duty as Dick Maney's associate, when I got to Philadelphia I relayed the information to my contact at the Ritz Carlton, Jack Hardy.

Jack couldn't contain himself, and neither could I. We were doubled up with laughter. Recovering from his mirth, Jack said he would arrange the requests even if it meant discombobulating his regular patrons by putting them in other rooms.

We both agreed it would be more fun to be able to watch the nocturnal perambulations that were to transpire with the manager on one side and the producer on the other, than the play we were representing. We could just see those doors slowly open, and then quickly close, as the two boys tiptoed into her boudoir. This whole scene would be worthy of a Feydeau farce (the French playwright who penned his farces in the late 19th and early 20th centuries) and one that would have brought more laughs than *Skin of Our Teeth.*

What really happened? Who knows, but I'll bet, once the boys found out that both had made similar requests they were both more than "discreet," and nothing happened. The producer/manager lust scene died aborning.

Maney's dislike of having to leave his Manhattan haunts grew more pronounced with the burdens of his company handling more and more plays. One day, one of his more insistent producers decreed that Dick go down to Washington, DC, not one of his "China boys," to drum up interest in the attraction. My boss reluctantly consented, and caught an early express to the Capital. He timed his visit in order to catch an express back that afternoon, allowing him but a few hours in Washington.

(I believe the term "China Boy" was invented because of my fellow associate, Hank Sember, who was known to Maney as "Togo" due to his squat contour and Oriental caste. Dick lumped us all together and came up with the term. Jack Toohey, Hank Sember, and I were his coolies, his slaves, his "China Boys.")

Jay Carmody, drama critic of the *Star*, one of Maney's best friends, was so miffed at the brevity of Maney's visit that he and the manager of the National Theater, Scott Kirpatrick, plotted revenge for "the slight."

Carmody noted in his column, "The eminent publicist, Richard Maney, showed up in town yesterday for half an hour on behalf of his attraction, the name of which I didn't catch, that has been booked into the National Theater in the near future."

Carmody had the compositor pull a proof, circled the barbed paragraph and then sent it over to the National Theater. Scott had it blown up and put in the lobby the following Tuesday, the day of Maney's next visit to Washington. Scott lashed it to the entrance door so that Maney couldn't miss it.

Of course, kind hearted Carmody saw that the paragraph was deleted before the column ran in the paper the next day.

It was a fine idea as a practical joke, but alas it missed its mark. I had been deputized to show up that Tuesday and stay a while working on the show. Maney never saw the jibe.

A press agent's cardinal rule: get your clients' pictures in the papers as much as you can, not yours, and that goes for articles, too. So when *Life Magazine* devoted a full article to Richard S. Maney and his place in the Broadway sphere, his China Boys couldn't resist. They had the ad agency blow up the article with a new headline: "How About Getting the Clients' Names in the Papers, Mister!" We then hung it in the office. Our boss loved it.

Maney had strong attachments to the principles of Christianity given to him by his Irish immigrant parents, but had a $20^{th}$ century man's irritation with some of the Roman Catholic hierarchy. When he married a divorced woman, Maryland –bred Betty Stoddard, and raised her son, Jock, Jr. as his own lad, he left the church for good. However, I did notice a rosary wasn't too far from his typewriter in his top drawer.

On occasion, Maney liked to carouse with the boys at the local watering hole. On one particular occasion, Maney was entertaining some of his out-of-town cohorts and wandered back to his apartment house in the wee hours. Meeting his son, Jock, in the lobby he queried, "Where are you off to at this ungodly hour?" Jock meekly replied, "I'm on my way to school, Father."

Dick's verbal venom was usually launched at superiors on the social scale. I recall his irritation at the management of the St. James Theater when he discovered the charwomen were miserably underpaid. He told off the management in no uncertain terms and won a raise for the cleaners. At the time, Dick was handling a hit at the theater and knew the take at the window. Another of his pet peeves were the less than square-shooting Shuberts, whose business practices would curl any bank examiner's hair not to mention the Justice Department. If there was a shoddy way to cheat anyone, the Shuberts not only knew it, but put it into practice. This was far different from the Shuberts'

Organization of today and its forward-looking methods.

Dick had his own personal filing system but he could always locate a story. "Things to do" he scribbled in brief notes to himself and put them in his left hip pocket. "Things done" he placed in his right hip pocket. At the end of a busy day, he would empty his pockets and see what needed doing. "Things done," he would file, "Things to do," he would act upon. He defied organizers or computers of any kind. His system worked well for him.

As Otis Guerney reported in his "Best Plays Summation of 1966-67," "It was the season that saw The *Herald Tribune*, The *Journal American* and the *World Telegram & Sun* go under."

It no doubt hastened Dick Maney's determination to fold his tent. He did it quietly, simply locking the door of his office and going home to Fairfield, Connecticut. He wrote his incredulous Broadway friends and associates, of which he had many:

"Of course I 'm going to miss the theater. But at 75 plus, I thought it the better part of valor to go AWOL while I still had a few of my marbles. If I had learned anything in the theater it is that everyone stays too long: playwrights, musical saw players, acrobats and David Merrick. I'm one of the theater's fortunate. Rarely have I been idle for more that a week or two in the last 40 years. Few stars can make such a boast. I raise my glass to you, Sirs!"

That quote is so Maney, a gallant to the end!

Dick's office in the Playhouse, when he finally gave up as a publicist to retire to his beloved Betty, her horses, and his bucolic pleasure in Fairfield, should have been carted intact, with its framed window card, the enormous desks, filing cabinets, beat up manual typewriters and scrapbooks, to the Museum of the City of New York. It should have been labeled; this was the way a press agent's office looked in the Twenties through the Sixties.

The production that crowned Dick's career, *My Fair Lady,* was a fitting end to a distinguished and fun-filled life.

*Scene* **7**

*"Salutes"*

Dick's office allowed us some enormously creative outlets as press agents. I believe my best work for "The Master" was originating some network radio special events, usually with the press staff from WOR and the Mutual Network who were next door to our office at 40$^{th}$ and Broadway. Alvin Joseph, Lester Gottlieb, Dave Driscoll were all stage struck, and eager to cooperate.

The programs were usually in the form of "a salute," and were booked to air immediately after the 11:00 PM news program when, in the halcyon pre-early WWII days, the Mutual Network of the Mutual Broadcasting system was running third and fourth behind the Red and Blue networks of NBC and ABC, owned and operated by RCA. If you can remember WEAF or WJZ in New York City, you'll recall those days clearly.

"The Corn is Green," Emlyn Williams' autobiographical play about a school teacher who helps a Welsh miner become educated and take his Oxford exams despite the opposition of the local squire, was a natural for "a salute."

This fine Herman Shumlim production was building up for an unusually long run on Broadway, with Ethel Barrymore in the lead role, making the comeback of her great career.

The first special event was a two-way program to London, which was a tear-jerker if ever one was conceived. Emlyn had sent his beloved wife, Molly, and the boys to the country when the Battle of London was in full swing. He felt the need to stay in London.

Ethel Barrymore, Richard Waring, Mildred Dunnock and the whole cast came to the studio after the performance at the National Theater, now called the Billy Rose Theater, and played a scene and sang for Emlyn who, in the early hours of dawn, sat at an open mike at the British Broadcasting Company's studio in London. Ethel and Emlyn played a scene from Emyln's play with Miss Barrymore sitting at her mike at WOR in New York City, and he in London.

The hour-long program ended with Molly, Emlyn's wife, talking to her husband by phone from the country and wishing him "Godspeed." The fire bombs and rockets had been bad that week.

To us pro-Allies, it was a terribly moving and brilliant program. It sounded like a carefully rehearsed prime time show, which it wasn't at all.

The show went over the wires live. In those days there was no such thing as taping a show.

What was the cost for doing the show? Shumlin was billed by the telephone company for an international call.

I proposed another of my ideas to Maney; that we get a network show lined up to celebrate Ethel Barrymore's 40th year of stardom and include her two brothers, John and Lionel, who were living in Hollywood. I was big on two-way programs, a technical feat in those days, and it would mean hooking-up the Hollywood brothers with sister Ethel who was in New York City.

Maney got hold of Miss B's agent, Bill McCaffrey, at the William Morris Agency. Bill thought the idea was super and believed it deserved the network with the most stations and the highest ratings. If they were going to produce the three Barrymores on one program they had to go for the big time and, can you imagine, the Barrymores were going to do this for free!

Well, it took a lot of dickering with Metro Goldwyn Mayer, then the top of the heap, as they controlled John's and Lionel's contracts for radio and everything else.

The program not only came off, it was triumphant but for one problem, a minor item. Louis B Mayer, the mogul and the Mayer in the movie giant, Metro-Goldwyn-Mayer, insisted that if he released Ethel's two brothers for the show, that plugged the stage play *The Corn is Green,* which the Warner Brothers, MGM's competitors, had recently won the rights to produce the movie version staring Bette Davis, Mr. Mayer had to be included in the radio program.

Mayer had his time in front of the mike but his poorly delivered paean of praise for Ethel's forty years brought snorts of derision from Ethel as she sat at her desk at NBC's Studio 9C. Flanking her were the likes of Lillian Hellman, Dorothy Parker, and Arthur Hopkins (who produced John Barrymore's famous *Hamlet*)

Again we did a scene from *The Corn is Green*. It was first-rate theater and radio. And despite its late hour, 11:15 to midnight, Eastern Time, it had a fine reception.

Walter Winchell of the New York Daily Mirror who had the best syndicated column of any New York Columnist in those days, reported in 2000 newspapers worldwide with 50 million readers. I wrote about the estimable Miss Barrymore and her career, sent it to Walter and I was pleased that he printed it verbatim.

None of these did anything but help the subsequent national tour of *The Corn is Green* and the film that followed. It was the best kind of publicity because it was about remarkable talents, and the nature of the program celebrated the best of the theater. It stood head and shoulders above the usual fare. It was first rate, just like the Barrymores, Emlyn Williams and Herman Shumlin. I felt proud of being a part of such a wonderful celebration.

Another "salute" of which I was proud was for Canada Lee. Mr. Lee was Broadway's newest black actor playing in the Orson Wells-staged play, *Native Son.* Again it was with WOR-Mutual.

On the east coast we lined up all the best black talent we could find to help salute our newest black star. W.C. Handy brought his beat-up horn and played his famous "St Louis Blues." Richard Wright, the novelist-playwright was there along with Paul Robeson, the eminent singer. From the west coast, Duke Ellington played his newest work; Eddie Anderson, popularly known as Rochester in the Jack Benny show, added a light touch; and Hattie McDaniel, of "Gone with the Wind" fame, added drama.

In those pre-tape recorded days it all had to be live. When it came to the brief get together with the director, Bob Shayon, Robeson said, "My accompanist and I have already rehearsed at home," indicating that "You won't have to worry about our performance." He continued, "Just give us eight minutes."

Robeson came on near the end of the show. His song, delivered with that marvelous timber-shaking bass, shattered all of us. "Why Does the Black Man Ride Alone?" The ballad was a protest against American Apartheid, and it hit the mark. The southern end of the Mutual Network started disconnecting the show right across the Sun Belt. It said something about the effectiveness of Robeson's shot.

Radio was wide open then because it was less commercial, uncluttered with today's lucrative and idiotic "messages." Commerce hadn't reared its ugly head with today's ad-crazy medium. It was Fred Allen who later said of TV and it might, too, have been added to today's radio, "I know why it is called a medium. Nothing is well done."

*Scene* **8**

## *Maurice Evans, English Import*

Maurice Evans was born in England and was ten years my senior. He started his serious acting career in London in 1927 and by 1934 he was a fixture with the Old Vic Company, appearing in many Shakespearean plays. His most notable Shakespearean role was that of King Richard III.

Katharine Cornell and Guthrie McClintic made routine trips to England seeking acting talent for their troupe and on one such trip to London they spotted Maurice Evans, a rising star. Knowing that Evans would add a great deal to their organization, they asked him to join them in America to play the role of Romeo opposite Mrs. McClintic as Juliet in Shakespeare's *Romeo and Juliet.* Not fully comprehending, Evans asked one of his friends, "Who is this Mrs. McClintic?" His friend berated him for his ignorance and retorted, "She's only

Katharine Cornell, one America's most famous actresses!"

And that began Maurice Evans' long and fruitful life in the American theater, as successful actor, director and producer.

It was a year after the end of the war that my relationship with Maurice began; he asked me to be the press agent for a revival of *Man and Superman,* by George Bernard Shaw. I was pleased to be asked especially with my attachment to and interest in Shaw's plays. Remember, I was the one who had started the yearly festival of Shaw at the Hedgerow Theater in the early 30's. And Evans' assignment came at an opportune time; Lewis Harmon and I had recently set up our own shop. I now had my own agency.

We opened in New York in the Fall of 1947 and the play ran for 294 performances, a successful run in anyone's book. Maurice was amazing; he starred as the lead role of John Tanner and was also the director and the producer of Shaw's play.

*Man and Superman* is in four acts and is very long and wordy, as is typical of Shaw's plays. Fortunately, Evans shortened the show by omitting the third act "Don Juan in Hell." Daughter Judy, who I took to see the play, reminded me of this omission.

With this booming success, Evans went on to produce a series of plays, but the next one in which I was involved, five years later, was a complete bust. It was *Wild Duck* written by Henrik Ibsen, who was known as "the Godfather of Modern Drama," and it was adapted for the stage by Max Faber.

Not wanting to begin our run cold on 55$^{th}$ street in Manhattan at the City Center, we elected to try the show out in Hartford, at the Parsons Theater (which has since been torn down). We hoped that a week in Connecticut would smooth out the rough spots.

On opening night in New York, after the final curtain, I went downstairs to Maurice's dressing room and I guess I don't have much of a poker face. Maurice took one look at me and said, "Oh, my God, Sol. Were we that bad?" I didn't have to reply. *Wild Duck* closed after 15 performances.

A year later it was a different story. *Tea House of the August Moon* was a booming success.

While he was trouping in 1951, Maurice read the novel "Tea House of the August Moon" written by Vern Sneider and, although the plot is pretty thin, Maurice thought it had potential as a play if it were re-written. Maurice was a savvy enough business-man to purchase the rights to the play and have John Patrick adapt the Snieder novel into what became the 1953 Broadway play.

Previous to our opening, The *New York Times* ran a large spread on October 11$^{th}$, featuring *"Tea House of the August Moon*, in their Sunday Drama Section. Once again my friend, Al Hirschfeld, created one of his magical caricatures of the show, including the goat.

It is unusual that a goat gets prime time publici-ty but Saki was no ordinary nanny goat.

*Mariko as Lotus Blossom and David Wayne*
*as Sakini, who is offering her with other gifts from the*
*community to Captain Fisbe.*

132

*John Forsythe as Captain Fisbe, and the goat, Saki.*

The scene is in the second act: the villagers had concocted a brandy and were worried that the newly fermented liquid might be lethal. They decided to try it first on the goat. If she keeled over, well, that would answer their question. Once a night Saki would eagerly drink the questionable "brandy" (which was really Coca Cola, Saki's favorite) and obviously live through the experience. The expression on Saki's face, as she licked her chops, made the audience go wild.

Saki was housed on 66th Street along with the Central Park's array of carriages and horses. Two hours before show time, her trainer and owner, Mr. Burns, would hail a taxi outside her stable and together they would travel to The Martin Beck Theater. It was quite a sight for New Yorkers to see a goat riding in a cab. When the cab had to stop at a red light and revealed Saki inside, there were many who thought they had had one too many drinks.

*Tea House of the August Moon* opened on Oct 15, 1953 and ran for 1,027 performances. It was a Broadway hit, winning many awards including: the New York Drama Critics Circle Award for Best American Play of the Year, the Pulitzer Prize in Drama and the Tony Award. The show starred David Wayne, Paul Ford and John Forsythe.

The play takes place in the tiny town of Tobeki on the Island of Okinawa following WWII, during the American occupation. It shows how we Americans try to impose our culture on others not knowing or not caring about the customs of that country.

Captain Fisby is assigned to the town by his commanding officer, Colonel Purdy, with orders to Americanize the town using plan "B." Fisby held elections, and a Mayor, Chief of Police and President of the Ladies League for Democratic action are duly elected. Plan "B" also calls for the building of a schoolhouse which just happens to be a pentagon in shape. Capital has to be raised and Fisby tries to market Tobeki's local handmade products such as sandals, cricket cages and straw hats. Discovering there was no market for these items, Fisby turns to sweet potato brandy, a product close to the hearts of Tobekians. The Cooperative Brewing Company of Tobeki churns out brandy by the gallons and becomes quite profitable, thanks to the drinking habits of the neighboring military bases.

However, as a democracy, the officials of Tobeki decide it is a teahouse that they wish to build, not a schoolhouse. Captain Fisby, captivated by the beauty of the Tobeki culture and their slower way of life, agrees to their wish. Of course, his decision has nothing to do with his gift from the village of a lovely geisha girl named Lotus Blossom.

On the opening day of the teahouse, Colonel Purdy arrives to make an inspection and is dumbfounded to find that a teahouse was built instead of a school and that brandy was their income source. He orders both the stills and teahouse demolished. The villagers cleverly only pretend to destroy all, but instead hide everything "quick as the dickens." All ends well when Colonel Purdy learns that

Congress is about to use Tobeki as a model for the success of Plan "B" and the teahouse is quickly rebuilt on stage. Fisby becomes a hero and, hopefully, Colonel Purdy will become a brigadier general.

Although cricket cages were not profitable for the Tobeki community, they were for us. The cages were quite popular as souvenirs with our audience.

Maurice hated to spend money unnecessarily. Such was the case when he learned that he needed 20 white jackets for the last scene in the play, the grand opening of the teahouse. He was told that the short coats would run into the thousands of dollars. Maurice refused to sign off on the expenditure and insisted there had to be a cheaper way.

One day while traveling by taxi back to his lower 10th street Westside apartment, he spotted a "Good Humor" truck. After alerting his taxi driver that he needed to talk to the driver, Maurice rolled down his window and shouted "Mr. Good Humor-man, excuse me, I need to talk with you. Where did you buy your white jackets and how much do they cost?" Answering both questions, the ice-cream man told him, "They cost $20.00 each and we get them from a local distributor and I'll write down their name for you." And that's how, for $ 400.00 and not thousands, Maurice costumed his cast.

The bane of many a press agent is when the producer, while the show is out of town, decides that the title is all wrong and a new one has to be invented. That happened to me when Maurice Evans called me from Boston to say that *Double Bill,* the

Terence Rattigan show consisting of two plays, *Harlequinade,* a farce, and *The Browning Version,* a drama about a college professor and his unsatisfied bride, was not drawing well at the box-office despite the fine notices from the critics. Maurice was starring in the shows opposite the famous actress, Edna Best. Evans decided to drop what he considered a confusing title, *Double Bill,* and substitute for it, *The Browning Version.* For me that meant that all the printing had to be dumped and rewritten, the ads reworked, and the stories changed, all of which I did, reluctantly. I knew that it was unlike Mr. Evans to spend money needlessly, so I didn't protest the change. The play opened at the Coronet Theater, now the Eugene O'Neill Theater, in 1949 to fine reviews. But under its new title it did no better than it did under *Double Bill.* It folded after 62 performances. I suspect the canny Mr. Evans realized afterwards that it was the subject of the material that did not interest the audience. Maurice Evans and Edna Best were brilliant in their roles.

Mr. Evans was a rare showman and never kidded himself, especially about box-office figures. He could read a statement with the smartest managers in the business and knew what to look for in the advance sale of tickets, or the date when it was profitable to close the show and move on. Evan's lack of false modesty, or ego, was refreshing and was a quality he shared with the star-manager who had brought him to these shores, Katharine Cornell.

Trying to persuade Maurice to be a guest on the show "Information Please" was a case in futility.

The show was one of the more literate programs on the air with Clifton Fadiman as the M.C. who asked a panel of guests to answer questions on various topics.

I caught Maurice in his dressing room and broached the subject; would he be a contestant on the famous show?

"Not on your life, Sol." He went on, "They will ask me to identify quotes from Shakespeare and, after all these years and productions, I can't tell one from the other. They all sound alike."

*Scene* **9**

*Female Flacks*

If it were up to Broadway, the Equal Rights Amendment would have had easy sledding. The publicity side of the commercial theater welcomed gals in my time.

I recall a photo during the early years of our union when five members picketed a reserved seat movie theater on Eighth Avenue which had refused to settle for a female union manager. The pickets were all press agents, all women. The ladies, top earners, were Helen Deutch, later author of the "Carnival" and other film classics, Frances Simon, Phyllis Pearlman, with whom I worked as an associate press agent, Elise Chisholm, and Jean Dalrymple. All were wearing their minks while parading on the line. The caption under the picture read, "Minks on the Picket Line."

Elsie Chisholm, a blonde, bright-looking gal and fashionable woman, worked for Dwight Wiman.

Helen Deutch, before she headed for Hollywood had more accounts than Richard Maney, and prestigious ones like Guthrie McClintic and Gilbert Miller.

Jean Dalrymple had her own flackery on East 42$^{nd}$ Street. A former actress, with startling good looks, she was much beloved by some editors and publishers in high places and was reputed to have had liaisons with several.

She later devoted her considerable talents to City Center, located on 55$^{th}$ Street, which she helped found along with John Golden and, during those early years, she was the Center's spokes- person. I worked with her for a few months as an associate and found she had so many clients that each associate had a list of them posted on the wall above their typewriters.

She favored baby-blue tinted paper for releases; distinctive, I thought.

The press woman I worked most closely with was Phyllis Perlman, who was senior publicist for George Abbott. Our office on the 18$^{th}$ floor of the RCA Building, overlooked the skating rink.

Phyllis, a graduate of The Columbia School of Journalism, was the wife of another press agent, Theron Bamberger, who became the producer of the Bucks County Playhouse in New Hope, PA, for a period of ten years, starting in the 1940s.

The year that I was under her wing, thanks to her motherly interest in me and my young family, I learned much, including better spelling habits. My father had always been upset that I could not spell properly and even went to the trouble of sending me a spelling book while I was at Camp Idlewild in the Adirondacks at Schroon Lake. The senior Jacobson believed I would never succeed in business without this necessary ingredient. Little did he know how many journalists never spell correctly, and depend entirely on their copy desks for corrections in both grammar and spelling.

Phyllis never typed without a cigarette dangling from her lips and she never bothered to remove it for a puff. How she kept the smoke out of her eyes was a minor miracle to me. I never had that problem with the pipe I smoked.

Our boss, Mr. Abbott, never master-minded his press agents; he concentrated on producing and directing his plays. We figured because Mr. "A" was a non-smoker, our barrage of billowing smoke fumes deterred him from invading our premises.

I only worked with Phyllis for less than a year but we became life-long friends and she would be a frequent visitor to our New Hope house on Windy Bush Road.

As a press agent, I was lucky when in Chicago, I had Gertrude Bromberg front my shows. Gertie, as she was fondly known, was house agent for the Shuberts in Chicago. In those days the road companies were produced with care to achieve a run just as long, if not longer, as when they were produced in New York. Chicago's Loop was often more profitable than any other outside New York City. When I first started my many years on the road, I was fortunate to have Gertie take me in tow and show me the ropes.

Later Gertie went out on her own and while she preferred shows that settled down in her home town, Chicago, she was not adverse to high-tailing it to the coast and back. And blessed was the show that Gertie's vast experience brought to it. She missed not a trick. She was thorough, bright and devoted to her job.

Another press agent that I especially enjoyed was Mary Ward, who had originally been an actress. Out of Kentucky, a born lady, in private life she was Mrs. Sayre Crawley. Mary met her husband-to-be, Sayre, when they were actors in the Civic Repertory Theater; the two fell in love and married.

Mary turned press agent when Eva LaGallienne, founder of that landmark Theater (Civic Repertory Theater) realized she needed the services of an "in-house" press person, rather than someone from "uptown." Eva wanted an agent who could get the message across of "repertory," that is, a different show each night. Mary fit the bill and became that person.

No one ever exuded optimism or integrity more than thin, bright, bubbling Mary. Her husband, Sayre, who played in *The Corn is Green*, as a senior scholar in Miss Barrymore's classroom, was just as sweet and loving as his wife. They made an adorable couple, as comfortable with each other as old shoes. When Sayre died, Mary took to the road as a publicist; the road was something she knew well from her acting days.

Among those who benefited most by Mary's decision to take to the road was Julie Harris. For many of her plays, Mary was her advance person. No more devoted or thorough press agent ever represented an actress unless it was Ray Henderson with Katharine Cornell. Details, such as to where to stay, the best places to eat were part of Mary's prepared list and, when Julie's son, Peter, came along, to where his nurse should wheel him. Of course these were added to the main chore, making sure La Harris' arrival in town was well known by the press.

When the youngish-looking 70 year old, Mary, died in New York on her way to the theater, many of her friends got together and raised a fund in her memory. Her favorite charity, for which she worked when she could spare the time, was the United Negro College Fund. It was the beneficiary of her memorial.

One of the most inventive bits of flackery was achieved by Helen Deutch in her working days. At the time, the Pulitzer Prize Committee was administered by an anonymous group of "experts" appointed by Columbia University, and it was rather conservative in its choice of a winner. Prizes had not proliferated and the Pulitzer Prize meant something at the ticket window. Maxwell Anderson was the poetic darling of Broadway in those days, or at least to producer McClintic, who was represented by publicist Helen Deutch. Anderson's *Winterset* ran to rave reviews and included a star-studded cast of Burgess Meredith, Margo and Richard Bennett. Also included was one of Joe Mielziener's most glorious stage settings; the scene of under the arching Brooklyn Bridge.

When the Pulitzer Prize Committee bypassed *Winterset* for the show *The Old Maids,* an adaptation by the American playwright Zoe Atkins from Edith Wharton's 1925 novel "The Mother's Recompense," Helen corralled her pals on the theater desks; Why didn't they form themselves into a Drama Critics' Circle and give their own award and show those stodgy old men up at Morningside Heights, a thing or two?

Dick Watts, Brooks Atkinson, Burns Mantle, John Mason Brown, Richard Lockridge, John Anderson, Robert Garland, Walter Winchell and Arthur Pollock; these were men of an independent cast of mind. Sure!

It was suggested that this august group meet at the Algonquin Hotel. Helen saw to it that her pal, Frank Case, the proprietor, oblige with a room and refreshments. An hour later they emerged with a constitution, which Helen typed up for them after taking copious notes. And they made their first Drama Critics' Award; you guessed it, Helen Deutch's show *Winterset.* The Year was 1935.

The following year, the committee met again and once again awarded a John Anderson's play, *High Tor* that had been overlooked by Pulitzer.

Katharine Cornell, Guthrie McClintic's wife played the lead role.

As the Ladies Home Journal adage went, "Never underestimate the power of a woman; especially one like Helen Deutch."

*Tennessee Williams*

In 1943, when I was the publicist on a show we were trying out in St Louis, MO., a conversation with William Inge, the drama critic at the St. Louis *Star-Times* came to mind. "Sol," he said, "There is a guy writing plays in town about whom you are going to hear." "What's his name?" I asked. "Tom Williams."

In the mid-50s William Inge becomes famous in his own right, writing hit plays such as *Come Back Little Sheba, Bus Stop, Picnic, and The Dark at The Top of The Stairs*.

Little did I know at the time how famous Tom Williams would become. During my Army tour of duty his name would pop up and, by the time I arrived home, Tom, who had taken the name Tennessee because he thought that "Thomas L. Williams" sounded too everyday, was beginning to gain attention. The production of *The Glass*

*Menagerie* in 1945 began his road to fame, sealed by *A Streetcar Named Desire* in 1948 and then *Cat on a Hot Tin Roof* in 1955. Each of the latter two won him a Pulitzer Prize for Drama.

Incidentally, although *Battle of Angels* closed in Boston in 1941 and was a bust, Williams rewrote the play, calling it *Orpheus Descending*. It opened on Broadway in 1957 and was mildly successful.

My first contact with Tennessee was in the swimming pool at the St. George Hotel in Brooklyn. You would think that New York City would have plenty of fine pools in which to swim and it did, but there was something special about the St. George swimming pool. It was the largest pool around and it was cheaper. Both of us went regularly for the same condition. I wanted to exercise my bum leg, caused by the bullet wound I earned in the Army and Tennessee to exercise his bum leg which had been stricken with polio when he was a kid and caused him to limp.

It was director Margo Jones who tapped me as press agent for Tennessee Williams' play *Summer and Smoke*. Jones had worked with Tennessee Williams before co-producing *The Glass Menagerie*. Her influence on the American stage is well worth noting.

Margo Jones was born in Livingston, Texas in 1911, my senior by a year. Interested in the theater, she worked in professional and community theaters in California, Texas and New York and traveled the world looking for innovative ways to present the theater. This led her to launch the American regional theater movement which decentralized the theater beyond Broadway. In 1947, she established the first regional theater company with the opening of Theater '47 in Dallas, Texas, where she introduced the 'theater-in-the round concept in the United States.

*Tennessee Williams flanked by Irene Selznick on the left and Margo Jones on the right*

Tragically, she died at age 43 having been exposed to poisonous tetrachloride fumes from a newly cleaned rug in her Dallas apartment.

I worked *Summer and Smoke* in two tryout towns, Buffalo and Detroit, before bringing it to New York on October 6, 1948 to the Music Box Theater. Williams dragged *Summer and Smoke* out of mothballs in an attempt to revive it, hoping that the play would do well this time by riding on the coattails of *Streetcar's* success.

My job always started well before we took to the road and sometimes even before the play was cast. As press agent, I had to prepare articles for the newspapers by writing feature stories, focused on obtaining the largest audience we could, once we opened. Our first stop was Buffalo.

In Buffalo, at the Erlanger Theater, I saw a concerned Tennessee. Eileen Darby was my photographer and, as the curtain came down on opening night, it was standard practice to shoot publicity shots of the cast in each scene, while they were still in full costume. We would start at the finale and work backwards until all the scenes were done. This was SOP in those days; one publicity shoot on opening night and only one. It was too expensive to do more due to the double-time pay paid to the unionized stage hands.

Eileen, who was visibly eight month's pregnant, decided she could snap a better picture if she climbed up on the upright piano in the orchestra pit. Tennessee, who was watching the whole process, decided he would watch no longer. The vision of a pregnant woman falling off an upright piano was too much for him. He ran out of the theater.

During our second stop in Detroit we once again polished *Summer and Smoke* with rewrites, trying to strengthen it for its opening in New York.

I obtained a number of radio interviews for Tennessee. These went extremely well and were well received; he was articulate and very modest. We became good friends and I treasure the Rainer Maria Rilke book of poems he gave me.

The re-writes and polishing did little good for *Summer and Smoke*; it was not a success that year. It folded after just three months on Broadway. However, in 1952, thanks to more re-writes by Williams and Geraldine Page's smashing portrayal of Alma Winemiller, the unmarried minister's daughter, the play became a huge success in the off Broadway theater, Circle In the Square.

At age 34 I had some theories as to why this play failed. I felt that Margo Jones, with all her expertise and talent, forgot one important fact. Stars are needed to promote a play. They are the ones that bring in an audience. Just to feature a playwright, even one as famous as Tennessee Williams, isn't enough. However, a notable exception was *Death of a Salesman* which opened in 1949 with no stars, just great actors, each perfect for his/her role.

Case in point; Tennessee Williams' *Sweet Bird of Youth* opened in New York at the Martin Beck Theater on October 10, 1959. It ran for a little over a year and starred Geraldine Page and Paul Newman.

*Sweet Bird of Youth* was nominated for 4 Tony Awards, including Best Actress for Geraldine Page.

Elia Kazan tapped my services and we opened at the Locust Street Theater in Philadelphia. Paul Newman, a handsome devil, was an emerging star, as evidenced by the mass of people who waited to see him emerge from the stage door exit. Paul was amazing; at the same time he was playing *Sweet Bird of Youth* he was also making the movie *The Young Philadelphians,* written by Richard Powell, whom I knew well when he worked for the Philadelphia *Ledger* as a reviewer.

*Paul Newman and Geraldine Page*

To his credit, even though he was a busy young man, Paul Newman never missed a performance and that meant eight a week. We referred to him as the Iron Man.

Tennessee Williams was not one of these up-tight authors who were so difficult to work with. After opening night in Philadelphia as we celebrated at the Variety Club at the Bellevue Stratford Hotel, Tennessee asked Elia Kazan, whom we all called "Gadge", "If there is anything you want me to do with the script, re-write or whatever, I'd be glad to oblige." "No," said Elia, "I am happy with the script the way it is." (Kazan earned his nickname "Gadge" from the word "gadget" because he was the one to go to if you needed something fixed).

*Sweet Bird of Youth* was the last of Tennessee's plays with which I was involved, although we did see each other on occasion when he wintered in Key West where both of us had homes.

Tennessee Williams' demise was sad. As his plays began to flop, one after another, his substance abuse increased and his thinking became more and more irrational. I was furious with him after he fired his literary agent, Audrey Wood. Audrey had been with Tennessee from the beginning and gave her life blood to see that all his plays were successfully produced, starting with *Battle of Angels*. After her firing I cut off all communications with Tennesee Williams, and never spoke to him again.

Tennessee Williams died in February, 1983, in his room at the Hotel Elysee in New York. The police report suggested his death was caused by an overdose of drugs and alcohol. Other statements indicated that although he did O.D. on everything, his death was a fluke accident. Williams was a hypochondriac and kept taking needless medication.He continually used a nasal spray and his death was the result of the cap coming off the spray, logging in his throat and he choked on it.

## *Joseph Aloysius Flynn*

Thinking of Joseph Aloysius Flynn brings a warm smile to those who worked around this "leprechaun of the road." More than any other publicist of my time, he conforms to what the public think of when they conjure up a vision of a press agent. He was a character, loveable but different, all of which I can attest to.

I first met Joe when he came to Philadelphia. He was there to promote the Chicago Company's *Three Men on a Horse*, a George Abbott farce about a fellow who had an uncanny ability to pick a racehorse winner at the track if he did not personally place the bet. Hume Cronyn, a young Canadian actor just getting his start in show business, was the lead.

It was the final year for The Garrick Theater, located opposite The John Wannamaker Department Store on Market Street. The theater was scheduled to be demolished to make way for new office buildings.

Joe was determined to stave off The Garrick's fearful fate as long as he could, by devising every stunt he could conjure up. So, he hired a retired brewer's mare and mounted three stooges; Horace Greenley McNabb, who was his protégé, "Major" White, a friend of Mc Nabb's plus a local neighborhood vagrant. He placed them on top of the nag, costuming the three in cutaways and bowlers, and then the horse, with its riders, ambled down Market Street with signs promoting *Three Men on a Horse*. Should the reader miss the signs the boys were carrying, Joe drove his point home by other signage on the horse's ample rump. It advised the reader to get themselves to The Garrick Theater for "the laugh of a lifetime at the show, *Three Men on a Horse*." If that were not enough to attract attention, there was a follow up. A Buster Keaton–like little man, mournfully trudged up and down Market Street, Chestnut and Walnut Streets and then onto Broad Street at crowded business hours, clutching a barrel around his midriff, with his bare legs protruding. Around the staves of the barrel was the lettering, "I lost my pants laughing at Three Men on A Horse." Between the two stunts, Joe succeeded in clogging traffic and getting headlines and also extended the life of The Garrick for a few months.

No doubt, Joe was a character and a bit peculiar. A noticeable eccentricity was that he liked to stuff his pockets with his own notion of health foods; raw carrots, celery, turnips and radishes. At no particular time he'd pull these gems out and begin munching like a giant rabbit. Then he'd top the raw turnip or radish with a shake of salt from his cache of stolen cafeteria shakers.

The bottom line of any good press agent is to "paper" the theater. It is essential, for if there is no audience, the show folds, and the flacker is not only out of a job but is without a pay check. Good publicity is the key to success for any press agent. If the drama editors place good copy in their respective newspapers and, if you are lucky or creative, your piece might get on the front page.

Joe was one of the most creative of press agents. He was legendary to his colleagues, many of whom were envious of his achievements, and to the city desk and entertainment page editors.

Flynn, born in County Mayo, Ireland was brought to Philadelphia, PA, as an infant. I'd often hear him chant, "Oh, I'm from County Mayo and was sent for by J.J. Shubert when I was just a babe of two."

His father, a blacksmith in the Old Sod, took up the same work in South Philly when he came to this country, in order to support his family of four. Joe's father had hoped his son would follow in his footsteps but his mother, to whom he was devoted, thought him too frail and spindly for such an arduous profession. But, it didn't matter what they thought; fate was to decide.

The senior Flynn died at an early age and young Joe had to get a job to help support the family, two boys and two girls. He went to work at

Snellenbergs Department Store opposite the Reading Terminal on Market Street in Philadelphia. Luckily,

Joe's boss at Snellenbergs took a liking to his new worker and urged him to attend night school. A good student, Joe also learned shorthand and typing. Curiously, when he became a press agent, he liked to pretend he was an illiterate, referring to his fellow colleagues who ground out feature and by-line stories, as "writing agents."

Early on, Joe liked to fool around with magic tricks. He kept perfecting them, working with another Philadelphian, Frank Tinney, who was a comedian and magician on the Vaudeville circuit. His neighborhood buddies also helped and Joe gained experience as a magician by taking his act to the many social clubs in the area. He was good with sleight-of-hand. Those who knew him as a lad thought he well might have been a professional magician. That was not to be; Joe would end up as a publicist.

From Snellenberg's he migrated to an apprenticeship with Nellie Revell known at the time, as the "Queen of lady press agents." She represented Oscar Hammerstein I at his recently opened Hammerstein's Victoria Theater at 42$^{nd}$ Street and Broadway, known as "the crossroads of the world." Joe's typing abilities, plus the gift of gab he had honed in his magic shows, stood him in good stead as Revell's helper. She was a rigorous taskmaster; he a willing pupil.

In 1920, one of their early assignments was to promote the new Apollo Theater, a creation of the Selwyn brothers, Arch and Edgar. Situated around the corner from the Victoria Theater, between Broadway and 8th Avenue on W. 42nd Street, it would house musicals, plays and burgeoning films. It had a wonderful sloping balcony and perfect acoustics, but so did other theaters in those days.

The question that the Revell-Flynn team asked themselves was how they could offer publicity that would make the Apollo Theater different than the others, thereby landing it on the front page of the papers.

Plotting long and hard, they came up with a winner. The Apollo Theater would be the first in the nation to have a smoking lounge exclusively for women. It would be advertised as a lady's smoking lounge, not just a powder room.

They planned their strategy, carefully leaking their idea to the daily papers and trade journals. Having baited the trap, they then sat back and waited. They didn't have to wait long for the prim public fell for it like mice after cheese. In no time, preachers were sermonizing from their pulpits across the city about this "hell hole, this den of iniquity," where high class society could shamelessly exhibit their vices, where innocent maidens, in their mad strivings to be stylish, would sink to their lowest levels.

And the anger didn't stop there; the refrain was picked up and bellowed outside the city. Those who never heard of the Apollo Theater soon did and they got an earful. Editorialists joined the gentlemen of the cloth in decrying this latest pandering to low taste. And that's how the Apollo Theater got off to such a good start.

Another one of Revell and Flynn's brain children was how to promote a play that was to open at the Victoria Theater owned by Oscar Hammerstein I, grandfather of the famous Broadway lyricist. Their answer; use French balloonists who had recently come to New York. They hired the balloonists to travel down the Hudson River and land, with proper fanfare, in front of The Victoria, on Times Square. Preparations were made; Revell and Flynn had set up "stringers" along the route to spot the Frenchmen's progress and phone it in. All the city desks were alerted to the impending event.

But alas, the dashing Frenchmen had spent the night before their balloon ride with too much partying; they were unable to lift themselves out of bed, much less elevate their balloon.

It wasn't long before Flynn's phone began to ring off the hook; "Where the hell are those Frenchmen?" Phone call after phone call came with the same query.

"Hold it!" Flynn countered in the best Front Page tradition. "We just got a flash from Blauvelt, New York. The Frenchmen have been sighted over the Palisades. They've been attacked by 'Air Serpents'. Yep, that's right, 'Air Serpents.' There is a fierce battle going on. Hold on, keep the phone open; I'll fill you in."

The afternoon editions of the newspapers printed hourly reports of the battle of the French balloonists and how they vanquished the "Air Serpents."

When the balloonists sobered up and finally arrived at Times Square, they were hailed as heroes. Thanks to the publicity, the show at Hammerstein's Theater, was "In Like Flynn."

Joe often used variations on a theme when it came to his creative publicity. As in the Apollo Theater's smoke lounge for women where he aroused the wrath of the clergy, he concocted a similar stunt in Chicago. Enlisting the help of Peggy Doyle, who wrote articles for the Chicago American's entertainment section, the two cooked up a lively feature. This particular musical play was in its last days and needed a shot of adrenalin. In those strait-laced days, the girls in the chorus lines were corseted with tight laced bodices. The suffragette movement was growing, beginning to advocate votes for women and equal rights. Joe had his chorines hop on the bandwagon for liberation. His girls obliged with carefully prepared statements; "We will shed these corsets. And why not; male dancers in our chorus line don't need them, why should we? Down with corsets!"

Peggy wrote an eye-catching story and her editor, Walter Howey, obliged with a liberal display of "art" photos, especially posed to feature Flynn's dancers without corsets.

Again, the "Bluenoses" were thundering from their pulpits. "This dangling flesh is sinful, a lure to the worst instincts of man."

The box-office took off like a rocket and stayed elevated for the rest of the Windy City run.

Perhaps the stunt that Joe is best remembered for was pulled not on tour but on Times Square. He worked for the Shuberts for many seasons, and they would use him to publicize a show in New York and then send him out on tour across the county with the same production. In the pre-World War II days, few shows would run the length of time they do today. In those days if a play would run 100 performances, Variety, the magazine of Broadway, considered that a mark of success. The show then went on the road to garner additional customers. Transportation to New York City, from out of town, just didn't exist as it does today. Customers didn't fly in for the weekend to catch the latest shows on Broadway.

While on Broadway, Joe was the publicist for a revue, *Streets of Paris* which needed a kick in the pants. Putting on his thinking cap Joe cooked up a tug-of-war for the girls in his show against those of a rival one, *On Your Toes*. The setting; Times Square, where he knew a crowd would gather and he would get publicity.

In those innocent days, the standard garb for ladies of the chorus was one-piece bathing suits, stockings and high heels. It was considered pretty hot cheesecake in the pre-bikini era.

A goodly crowd gathered in anticipation and the girls took their stations on the rope, squaring off against each other. All was set to begin and Joe handed one of the girls in the cast a starter's pistol which he had borrowed from his prop man. Police on horseback held back the gawking audience, along with a goodly contingent of reporters and news photographers who were on hand to record the momentous event.

When the pistol went off to start the tug-of-war all hell broke loose. Panic ensued as the horses, startled by the noise from the starter gun, reared up on their hind legs and snorted, discombobulating their riders and panicking the crowd.

The police captain in charge became so incensed by the resulting melee that he issued a summons for the innocent actress who had fired the pistol. She had to appear in court but, fortunately, she was represented by the Shubert's counsel and the case was dismissed.

Joe Flynn had quietly disappeared, but not really; he just stayed out of New York City for a while until the whole story simmered down.

The tug-of-war Times Square Battle and the subsequent arrest, complete with photographs, graced the papers that afternoon and the tabloids the next morning. Joe viewed it all as a successful operation.

However, the police department kept after the Shubert press department, in particular Claude Greneker, its head, to track down the culprit. Joe was nowhere to be found. When the District detective tried to reach Flynn by telephone, the Shubert's operator taking the call advised the detective, "Flynn? Oh hell, we fired him. He probably went back to the Coast because he's all washed up here."

Joseph Aloysius Flynn's last years were spent with Horace McNabb in his rustic hideaway on Jericho Mountain in the rolling hills of Bucks County not far from New Hope, PA. Joe had been doing the advance work for *Most Happy Fella* in San Francisco when he phoned McNabb to say that he was feeling miserable and would have to pack it in. He was giving the management his notice, "throwing in the towel" as he put it.

"Why don't you come down and spend some time with me," suggested Horace. "I have a bunch of old friends living with me; we call it the geriatric Boys Town. Put your trunk on the train and fly in to Philly. I'll meet you," said his longtime disciple, then publicizing a shopping center near Levittown, PA.

McNabb continued; "He was happy in the country with me and stayed a year. I gave him a mutt, which I got at the local SPCA. The pooch was all white with a brown patch on his eye, and one of his parents must have been a boxer. Joe didn't want a dog, claimed it would keep him awake at night. But I knew he needed company when I went to work every day."

Joe's demise was in keeping with some of his other capers. He died in his hometown, Philadelphia, at the Jefferson University Hospital, just up the street from the Forrest Theater where he had worked many times. The medical staff gave him a shot of morphine and Flynn never came out of a coma, so he was unable to take last rites. It was his wish to be buried next to his beloved mother in a Catholic cemetery in suburban Yeadon.

When McNabb asked that his friend's wish be fulfilled he was informed by the funeral director that Joe's request to be buried in sacred ground would not be forthcoming. He had "refused" last rites, according to the undertaker.

"Now just a minute," roared Flynn's protégée. "Joe was too doped up to know what he was doing." Not getting anywhere with the undertaker, the grief-stricken McNabb called Milton Weintraub, the press agents' union secretary-treasurer. Milton calmed him down by saying, "Not to worry, Horace. I'll handle it." Milton in turn called his good friend Tommy Labrum, who was, at the time, head of the local chapter of our union.

If there was anyone who could accomplish miracles in Philadelphia it was LaBrum, the same man who suggested that if I wanted to get anywhere as a publicist I should move to New York City. LaBrum had the right contacts. He just happened to represent the newspaper publisher, David Stern plus John B. Kelly, a well known industrialist and civic leader in Philadelphia and the father of the famous actress, Grace Kelly.

When Tommy came on the phone in his usual soft, low-key fashion, he queried McNabb. "Kid, what show is in town?"

"*J.B*, Achibald MacLeish's show with Basil Rathbone as Job," answered Horace.

"Great. How many free tickets can you get for me?"

A fast telephone call to Maurice Turet, a fellow publicist who was handling the show, answered the question. Back to Tommy; "I can get 250 pairs for the following Monday night. Turet says it's slow and they were going to paper the show with nurses anyway."

"Get the tickets punched out at the box-office," advised LaBrum, "and send them over to Monseignor O'Brien at the Cathedral. Then call me back a half hour after their arrival, kid, that is a half hour after the tickets are delivered."

The next week Joe was buried with a High Mass in Yeadon. "A High Mass," mused the still incredulous McNabb when he was so informed by the Cathedral.

It was no wonder why the local diocese was not endeared to my friend Joe. He had an irreverent, bawdy streak. They remembered well when Joe had a poster of a lightly-clad chorus girl drawn for one of his shows. Her cheerleader stance had this lettering between her legs, "Special! Two Buck Matinee Today."

That's Joe for you!

When Joe Flynn died at the age of 72 in 1968, he left $50,000 to his protégé, Horace Greenly McNabb, other funds to a nephew and a $5,000 contribution to our union's welfare fund.

## *Drafted at age 32*

*A picture of our family just
before I was shipped overseas*

While working with the Maney organization I was assigned to Jean Dalrymple's office on a revival of George Gershwin's *Porgy and Bess*. The show had moved over to New York from its Maplewood, NJ tryout. It was a resounding hit with again many of the originals in the cast along with its creative musical director, Alexander Smallens.

In the late Spring of 1944 I was drafted into the US Army and assigned to a Rifle Division. Can you believe it? I was 32 years old, with a wife and two young children, and my education in shooting an M1 was nil as was that of most of the other inductees. Dick Maney couldn't believe this was happening, and I saw the head of the Induction Draft Board, as I knelt down to kiss my two little girls goodbye, turn away with tears in his eyes.

I could have won a deferment from military service had I listened to Jean Dalrymple's sage advice; she was worried about my growing family, Judy, eight, and Baby Babs, two. But Broadway didn't seem very important to me compared with what was happening in Europe. The Invasion was in the wind and, with my Jewish roots, I was disturbed about rumors of what was happening to the Jewish people in Europe. I felt my presence on the front might help if only in a small way.

I was slated to fill the day's quota for a Navy assignment. That didn't happen thanks to a newspaper pal in the induction center in Allentown, PA, who, "fixed or re-routed" my entrance into the infantry.

I'll have to admit that during my year and a half in the service, there were times when I thought "fixing" was not such a good idea.

My induction was in Doylestown, PA., followed by a quick trip through Camp Meade and then on to Camp Croft, outside of Spartanburg, S.C., for weeks of basic infantry training, including how to handle the M-1 rifle. My issued M1's serial number was 33836279 (That, like your dog-tag number, is something you remember all your life). Camp Croft was known as a Replacement Training Center and we, most of us selectees - that meant we were drafted - were known as "loss replacements," an appellation that hardly made us feel warm and fuzzy.

Cash was short for me in those days and a buck private's pay was hardly enough to buy a couple of packs of cigarettes. So, in the evenings, Bob Johnston, a fellow inductee from Philadelphia who had worked for the Philadelphia *Record*, and I managed to do some work for the local paper, The *Spartanburg Herald*, to earn a few extra bucks. We did it all; wrote headlines, read and edited copy. This income, along with my father's help saved the day. Actually, if it had not been for my father, my family would have starved to death.

While at Camp Croft I had written to Colonel Frank McCarthy, a fellow press agent, who had worked with me for George Abbott and now was an aide to General George C. Marshall. I suggested in the letter that it made much more sense to put me in front of a typewriter than on a front line. Could he help?

When his answer came back, it created quite a stir at camp: why was Private Sol Jacobson getting a communication from Supreme Headquarters?

Frank's answer; "Sol, sorry I can't do anything for you because all orders have been frozen in place due to the pending invasion of Europe (D-day would take place on June, 6th, 1944); however, I'll follow your career with interest."

The Army gave us a week's leave after our many weeks of training and I spent the time saying goodbye to my family. It was an anxious time for us, for we knew we would be shipped to the front as soon as our week was up.

We reported to Fort Dix, N.J. and embarked on the Queen Mary for northern Scotland. It was a crowded voyage, hardly a luxury cruise. There were 15,000 of us and, every twelve hours, they would rotate half of us from the decks, where they fed us, to the lower quarters, where we slept. I guess the outside air was supposed to keep our spirits up and our food down.

We landed at Prescott on the Sheffield River in northern Scotland. Already trains were waiting to take us to Southampton where we were to embark for France.

When we had landed in Scotland, I was asked by my fellow GI's, "Where the hell are we?" "See those sheds over there?" I said. "That's for scotch whiskey. We're in Scotland and they ship that whiskey all over the world."

As we went down the gangplank we were sur-rounded by Scottish kids —yelling, "You got any gum, chum?"

The need for fresh troops in Europe was so great there was no time to lose. We landed in Scotland one day and the next day we were in France. I didn't even have enough time to phone my English relatives.

Our landing craft discharged us on Omaha Beach. When I asked the sergeant in charge what division I was in he barked, "See that cemetery up on the beach? That's the 29th Division and you're the fresh meat." I was assigned to the 29th Division, the 115th Infantry, Company C. Captain Richardson from Hendersonville, N.C., was in charge along with Sgt. Weir. Both men were later killed in action. Unfortunately, in our theater of war the life of a soldier in the infantry was not a long one. Sgt Weir was hospitalized due to loss of an ear. But his hospital stay was brief; he ran away to rejoin his unit only to be killed in later action.

Fortunately, nobody was shooting at us because the Germans had retreated to St. Lo.

I scaled the 150 foot cliff but thought I'd never make it to the top with all the crap I had in tow. My M1 and all my sleeping gear, a knapsack and a mortar bag around my neck made me look like a fat pack horse.

We scoured the Calvados area of the Normandy Province searching for the enemy. The apple orchards were full of fruit and the boys helped themselves to what they thought were succulent apples only to find they were sour as hell. That's where the famous Calvados Brandy comes from and the apples are supposed to be sour, I told them.

In a few weeks we were sent by truck to the walled city of Brest on the coast, where the allies were intent on making it a deep water port. The Germans decided to take a stand, defending their submarine pens that were there. But they were getting walloped on two sides – the U.S. Air Force dropping bombs by day, and the British planes by night.

In late August, we got dumped in the hedge-rows outside of the city.

Hedgerows had existed for several hundred years in Normandy and divided the farmers' plots, with some involving areas as large as 100 yards square. The hedgerows had been built originally with rocks cleared from the fields and placed in rows creating walls. During the intervening centuries, vegetation grew between the rocks, producing bushes and trees with heights of five to thirty feet. They made excellent defenses for the French defending their territory. The hedgerows were formidable, making it equally difficult for an attacking army to conquer the area. Even Julius Caesar complained about them.

It was into the hedgerows that my buddies and I found ourselves with the German Wehrmacht defending while we were attacking, definitely a disadvantage to us. A typical engagement had opposing forces shooting at each other and exchanging grenades with only the thickness of the hedgerow between them.

We were fighting our way forward when I got plugged. I got caught up in one of the hedgerows thanks to that damn mortar bag around my neck. I was lucky; the bullet, although it messed up my leg, didn't shatter any bones in the process. GIs refer to this as a "million dollar wound." The Germans referred to it as a "Heimatsschues," – a shot that sent you home.

With a hole in my leg and a finger wound caused by shrapnel, ( I still have the scar on my finger which acts as a constant reminder of that experience) I remember lying on the ground on the battle field hoping that if I kept real still and played possum, the Germans might not shoot me again. To take my mind off my dire situation, I pulled from my pocket one of the books the book industry had provided to GI's. It was an exciting mystery and I read it while I waited for the medics to get to me. In retrospect, I often wondered what that medic thought as he came upon this soldier with a serious wound of the leg, shrapnel in his finger, reading a book.

They sent me to a field hospital where I was quickly evacuated to a distribution center in Broadway, England and then to the hospital in Axminster. (Curiously the surgeons on staff were all from Houston, Texas. The Army preferred to keep surgical units together, knowing that they would perform better if they knew each other.)

I remember waking up the next day and reading, "Paris has fallen". It was August 25th, 1944.

My rehabilitation started just as soon as I was able to walk comfortably on my bum leg. Axminster, a quaint, beautiful market town on the eastern border of Devon, was built on a hill overlooking the River Axe. It became my outdoor gym and provided me with much needed exercise.

As the Jewish High Holidays approached I was fortunate to find a synagogue in the neighboring town of Exeter. Located on Mary Arches Street, it had served the community since 1763 originally as an Orthodox synagogue. By the '40s it had changed to a Progressive Synagogue, a term used by the Europeans to describe the service and rituals to be anything other than Orthodox. In the United States we would define Progressive as Reform, Conservative or Reconstruction.

The Exeter Synagogue was small, nestled between two adjoining buildings. It was built with the Rabbi's lectern in the center and had a balcony where, traditionally, the women sat. It was here I spent the High Holidays enjoying services that I found were familiar to my Reform roots.

(It wasn't until I started my memoirs that I found out that the Exeter Synagogue was established by my biographer's distant relative, Abraham Ezekiel, and is the second oldest synagogue in Great Britain - small world!)

I was fortunate to be hospitalized in England, for I had relatives who looked after me. My mother was English and had come to America in 1903 as a sales representative for Appolinaris, a bottled water company that boasted of special mineral contents which would improve your health, (there must be some truth in what they claim for they are still in business today) at the St Louis World's Fair and later at the Chicago World's Fair. While in America she visited her London neighbor, who had moved to Harrisburg, PA, and fell in love with my father, Morris Jacobson. They were married in 1911 and I came along in 1912, when both were well into their forties.

During my four month's stay in England I visited my cousins, John and Bert Goldman, regularly during the daytime. Bombing was severe at night and not a good place to be and, like so many other English citizens, Cousin John was a fire marshal at night, trying to bring some order out of the chaos caused by the heavy bombing attacks by the Germans.

John, who owned a trade ad agency, lived on Golder's Green in Northwest London. One of their neighbors, whom they didn't see much of because he was so busy at the Hallstead Studio, was none other than Alfred Hitchcock.

An afternoon I will always remember was when Cousin John took me to the ever popular Savoy Hotel on a crowded Saturday afternoon and said to the maitre d', "I want the best table in the house for my wounded Yank cousin." I was impressed.

The Battle of the Bulge lasted from December 16, 1944 to January 25, 1945. As a last resort, the Germans tried to punch a hole in the allied forces lines and split these British and American Allied lines in half. The hope was to then encircle and destroy the Allied Armies. Most of the fighting took place in the Ardennes Forests of France, with heavy losses on both sides.

Fortunately the Germans' effort ended up as a Bulge, not a hole, but the need for more Allied troops during the battle was so critical that an order came down from headquarters to empty all the hospitals and send any soldier who could stand and fire an M1, to the front.

My leg wound had healed sufficiently, so, back to the front I went; however, they didn't know what the hell to do with me and I ended up in snipers' school in southern Holland.

"What the hell is a sniper," I asked. "You shoot at targets all day," I was told.

And I did. I shot at targets all day trying to hone my skills as a sharpshooter on the way to becoming a sniper. However, the only gun that the Army had at the time with a scope was the 1903 Springfield rifle, hardly what you would call the latest in firearms.

A few weeks after starting my schooling, I read a notice that my good friend and employer, Katharine Cornell and her entire entourage, would be entertaining the troops in a one night stand not too far from where I was stationed. Katharine was playing her famous role as Elizabeth Barrett Browning in *The Barretts of Wimpole Street.* The play was a favorite of not only mine but of the whole troop.

They were surprised to see me and not too comfortable that I had my Springfield over my shoulder. But their attitude changed when they found the gun was not loaded; then it was old home week and, to me, like being back on Broadway again seeing all my old friends.

Not only did I see all my good friends but learned some interesting facts about Katharine's tour.

It was General Marshall who asked Cornell and her husband, producer Guthrie McClintic, to entertain the troops in Europe through the auspices of the USO and the Special Services Division. Katharine said she was pleased to do so and *The Barrett's of Wimpole Street* would be the vehicle. The play is the story of poet Elizabeth Barrett's love affair and subsequent marriage to the poet Robert Browning.

However, the Army had different ideas. They were convinced that no GI would sit through three hours of drama about two middle-aged English poets and suggested that Ms. Cornell consider *Blithe Spirit*, the comic play written by Noel Coward.

Kit answered she would play *Barrett's;* if she were going to entertain the troops she wanted to bring them her best, and that would be *The Barrett's of Wimpole Street.*

The Army countered, by asking her to cut at least the love scenes as the play was much too long, especially for the men in uniform. Perhaps she should explain the play to her audience before her performance to avoid what the Army saw as an audience that would be rude, tasteless and ignorant.

Kit was adamant that the play be shown in its entirety with every degree of authenticity of the Broadway original. Her entire troupe backed their leading lady. Katharine had played the leading role of Elizabeth Barrett Browning hundreds of times. It was truly her best and most inspiring role. And I can vouch for that, having seen her in this distinctive role so many times. So can Brooks Atkinson who wrote on the opening night in 1931,

> "After a long succession of meretricious plays it introduces us to Katharine Cornell as an actress of the first order. Here the disciplined fury that she has been squandering on catch-penny plays becomes the vibrant beauty of finely wrought character.... By the crescendo of her playing, by the wild sensitivity that lurks behind her ardent gestures and her piercing stares across the footlights, she charges the drama with a meaning beyond the facts it records. Her acting is quite as remarkable for the carefulness of its design as

for the fire of her presence.... The Barretts of Wimpole Street is a triumph for Miss. Cornell and the splendid company with which she has surrounded herself."

At the first production in Italy, the Army was almost vindicated; there was a lot of disturbance by the troops during the first act but as the play continued, the cat-calls subsided. As explained by one of the actresses, Margalo Gillmore;

"It is true, then, we thought, they would go on laughing and it would never stop and the Barretts would go under a tidal wave of derision. But we were wrong. Kit and Guthrie were holding the laugh, just as if they had heard it a hundred times, not showing any alarm, not even seeming to wait for it, but handling it, controlling it, ready to take over at the first sign of its getting out of hand. It rose and fell and before it would rise again, Kit spoke. Kit had a shining light in her. With that strange sixth sense of the actor that functions unexplainably in complete independence of lines spoken and emotions projected, she had been aware of the gradual change out front from a dubious indifference to the complete absorption of interest. At first they hung back, keeping themselves separate from us, a little self-consciously, a little defiantly, and then line by line, scene by scene, she had felt them relax and respond and give themselves up to the play and the story, till at last they were that magic indivisible thing, an audience. 'We must never forget this, never,' said Kit. 'We have seen an audience born.'"

When the tour opened in Santa Maria, a small town near Naples, the G.I.s lined up for three hours before the show. A manager overheard a tough, burly paratrooper say to one of his buddies, "Well, what did I tell ya? Told ya this was better than going to a cathouse."

*Katharine Cornell as Elizabeth Browning, Brian Aherne as Robert Browning in The Barretts of Wimpole Street*

So successful was the tour that the Army extended it first for two more weeks and then to six months. One of their last stops was Paris. While there, Gertrude Stein and Alice B.Toklas asked to see the show but were told it was for enlisted personnel only. Not to be deterred, they disguised themselves as GIs and did receive admission.

The tour finished in London amid screaming German V2 bombs.

On her return to New York, Kit found hundreds of letters from soldiers who had seen her show, thanking her for "the most nerve-soothing remedy for a weary GI," and for having brought, "yearned-for femininity," reminding them that, unlike other USO shows, "a woman is not all leg," and for "the awakening of something that I thought died with the passing of routine life in the foreign service."

Camp was 15 miles away but the only way back was to bum a ride from some kind soul. I was on the road with my thumb in the air when serendipity hit. My old friend from Baltimore, Lew Azrael drove up in his jeep.

Lew, a handsome guy, was imbedded in the 29th as a war correspondent for the Baltimore newspapers and went in with his unit on D day. We had met in Harrisburg when I was a kid; he was romancing my cousin, Marenet Simms, and was one of my role models.

He couldn't believe his eyes and all he could say was, "Is that you, Sol?"

Lew wanted to know what I was doing as a buck private in the US Army carrying a '03

Springfield. I let him know my situation was not of my own choosing; I was drafted.

"How would you like to be editor of the 29<sup>th</sup> Division's paper?" He continued, "We just lost our editor. I think he was drunk as a skunk when he fell out of his jeep, busted his hip and was sent home."

It didn't take long for Colonel Tom Dukeheart, head of the 29<sup>th</sup>s' newspaper, to cut the necessary orders which read, "I want this man." That was all that was needed and, as luck would have it, that's where I spent the rest of the war, as editor of the 29<sup>th</sup> Division's daily newspaper eventually rising to the rank of Sergeant.

*I'm in the passenger's seat*

It was in this capacity that I got to know Bill Mauldin, the famous cartoonist and creator of the 'GI Joe" cartoons, featuring "Willie and Joe." We were both enlisted men.

To garner material for his "GI Joe" cartoons, Bill liked to bunk in with non-officers. I certainly qualified in that category; I was an overage PFC, former combat rifleman, who had been sent back to the front to rejoin my unit.

After landing in Normandy, the 29th had fought its way through Normandy, Brittany and Holland into Muchen Gladbach. Preparations were now under way for crossing the Rhine and finally linking up with the Russians on the Elbe River.

The PR department, a division of the G-2 Section, to which I was assigned, was billeted in an abandoned home. Its residents had fled from the hordes of Yanks and Brits then assembling in the Industrial Ruhr Valley. I was behind a typewriter turning out "Joe Blow" hometown stories about the 29th division men for their hometown newspapers. Occasionally correspondents would show up for information and a spot to bunk down for the night. I have to admit that they would rather stay in the officers' quarters, obviously the more "swanky" of the two. That's why it was so unusual that when Bill Mauldin visited, he insisted he stay with us GIs.

The week Bill stayed with us, drawing-board in hand, was a pleasant one, for spring was advancing and we enjoyed taking meals together outside in the backyard of our occupied home. Meals; perhaps that's the wrong word for heated-up C rations.

Suddenly, one afternoon while we were enjoying our C-rations, a Luftwaffe plane came over with a plume of fire trailing from its tail. Bill whipped out his pistol and began firing at it. The rest of us ran for our M-1s that were stacked in the house. By the time we emerged with our firepower, the plane was far gone, onto another target. Bill's comment, "That plane must have been on fire. Hope it doesn't damage any of us when he crashes."

We were so unfamiliar with planes that we hadn't realized that we were looking at the Germans' new jet fighter in action, quite unfamiliar to us groundlings.

Bill's gentle kidding of us in his famous cartoon with a GI hiding his eyes with one hand and shooting with his other at a wounded jeep irked our division's commander, Charles Gerhart, known to all of us as "Jumping Charlie."

"It was no way to represent the troops" he said, and ordered us to turn out a daily newspaper that would give more positive pictures of the real soldier.

We were in the Bremen-Bremerhaven sector and we had no trouble writing a daily newspaper, but where were we to get news print and men who could operate such a machine?

It is amazing, if pushed, how ingenuity wins out. Someone discovered a cache of newsprint that was to be used by the Chicago Tribune. They had planned to put out a European daily to rival the Herald Tribune's Paris addition. It never came to pass and we were given the newsprint. Now all we needed was a linotype machine, which we found in an old German North Lloyd steamship warehouse, and a printing press. The press became available and printing and linotype operators are not hard to find, especially when your division has 15,000 men. Two riflemen were released to us. We were ready to go. We consisted of yours truly, Lieutenant Elmer Blasco and an ex-Brooklyn Eagle reporter, Phil Siegel, plus our two operators. We were understaffed to say the least.

There was another problem; no wire service. What to do? Problem solved; on the second floor of our liberated printing shop we found a wireless radio which could pick up a signal from WGY Schenectady, NY, the General Electric Station. It meant taking dictation but it gave us the news from home which we needed.

A paper isn't complete without cartoons and we knew Jumping Charlie's thoughts about Bill Mauldin. I suggested the Army send me to London to beg the *Daily Mirror* to let us use their popular strip "Jane," in which a shapely damsel divests herself of her outer garments. I never got to London because, when The *Daily Mirror* heard that a U.S invasion division was in need, they gladly gave us their strip and its striptease comic.

That's when Bill joined up with us for the second time. Although he did not stay long, he was amused that Gerhart went to such trouble to provide an alternative to his "Willie and Joe."

I enjoyed my work as editor and I knew that as long as the Army was fighting the Germans there was no need to worry about losing my job. However, because the US was fighting two wars, our real concern was the possibility that we would be shipped to the Pacific Theater. Fortunately, the Atom Bomb stopped that.

I was discharged from the military in October 23$^{rd}$ of '45 and started to work once again for my mentor, Richard Maney.

For participation in War II, I was awarded The Combat Infantry Badge, and The Purple Heart along with all the ribbons that pertained to my campaign. I would later receive the Ordre national de la Légion d'honneur (Chevalier) from the French Government.

Although my wife Bobbie and daughter Judy were ecstatic at my return and greeted me with open arms full of affection, that was not true of my three year old, Babs. She screamed on seeing me in uniform and lashed out with her fists, pummeling my chest. Her actions suggested that I was some stranger from a strange land and had no business being in our New Hope house, kissing her sister and mother.

Such are the trials and tribulations of the home-coming soldier.

# ACT III

★   ★   ★

## Broadway and My Golden Years

## *Jacobson, Doll and Harmon*

In 1946 I made the decision to set up my own agency and invited Bill Doll and Louis Harmon to join me as partners. We were known as Doll, Harmon and Jacobson. We had an office, if you want to call it that, in The Hudson Theater at 141 W 44<sup>th</sup> Street, a second floor walk-up. It was a big old vault filled with old theater stuff and a small "count–up room" was attached with its large safe. This is where The Hudson Theater kept its daily receipts and records. We squeezed in three desks, a phone line with two extensions, and typewriters for which we paid only $60 a month. As we were just starting out, we were thankful to our landlords, Lindsey and Crouse, for renting us anything. The location was just half a block from Broadway's theater district and worth a million dollars. In the beginning business was tough to come by.

The Hudson Theater had an interesting history: in the early 1900's, theatrical producer Henry B. Harris built a magnificent, four-floor luxury theater in the residential neighborhood of West 44th Street. It opened with Ethel Barrymore starring in *Cousin Kate*. Henry and his wife, Irene, ran a successful theater business for years. Unfortunately, Mr. and Mrs. Harris found themselves on the Titanic on that fateful day in April of 1912. A sad story followed. Irene Harris, with a bum leg caused by the iceberg collision, was carried by her husband to the last lifeboat. As the lifeboat pulled away from the sinking vessel, they waved a final goodbye. Four months after returning to New York, Irene decided she would run The Hudson Theater alone and became the first female owner and operator of a New York theater.

In 1929 she was offered a million dollars for her property, turned it down and, by 1933, The Hudson was in receivership. During the next eight years it changed ownership 18 times before being purchased by Lindsey and Crouse.

Bill Doll came from West Virginia and had the drawl to go with it. He had just finished his run as press agent for producer Alex Yokel's *Three Men on a Horse*. Bill was a wonderful guy but drank too much. He had recently gotten married and resided, with his new bride, in a cheap apartment across the street from our office. It was here, in his love nest that even during working hours, he spent most of his time. That's why Mike Todd had such a difficult time trying to contact him.

In the early '40s, Mike Todd, the same Mike Todd who at one time was married to actress Elizabeth Taylor, was working as a young shoe salesman at the Florsheim store on Michigan Avenue in Chicago, when he placed a call to Bill Doll. Mike had recently purchased the rights from "The Federal Theater Project" to produce *The Hot Mikado*, a musical theater adaptation of Gilbert and Sullivan's *Mikado,* to be performed by an all black cast. The musical was running in Chicago and Mike wanted Bill Doll to be his agent when it opened in New York.

Mike was working at the time, but during his break he'd go to the back of the store to make his calls to our office. And there were many calls, but to no avail. We repeatedly told Bill there was a guy in Chicago who wanted to talk to him; call him back. We finally realized that "love" had superseded work. Frustrated, I'd finally had enough and went across the street and banged on his door and then left the following note, "Get out of bed. There is a guy in Chicago who wants to give you a job." The call was finally made and Bill Doll took the job as Mike Todd's exclusive agent and we lost one of our partners.

*The Hot Mikado* ran successfully on Broadway. To publicize the play, Bill, very cleverly, had the whole cast dance down Broadway with Bill "Bojangles" Robinson, the star of the show, leading the way.

For the rest of our lives our Agency would be known as Jacobson and Harmon and we worked well together and became good friends. Unfortunately, during our twilight years, Louis became exceedingly deaf and the only way to converse with him was on the phone. You don't realize what a cut off not hearing is, until you have to work with someone who is hard of hearing.

Once I became an agent on my own, I made a conscious decision from which I never varied for the rest of my working career: I would never take a job as an exclusive agent. Although I was asked many times to do so, my answer was always no and for good reason. I enjoyed the summers off; that's when, as a family, we could travel together and we did, probably visiting every National Park in the US. If I was limited to being "X's" press agent solely, I could hardly pick and choose what I wanted to do. If I didn't like the show and wanted out, it was just too bad, or if I wanted to do something else, too bad. Exclusivity equated to indentured servitude as far as I was concerned. Being my own man gave me a much looser schedule and allowed me the opportunity to do other than Broadway plays and musicals, such as representing dance companies, or concerts or what have you. It also proved to give me a much more rounded experience. And most important it allowed me more time with my family.

My association with Louis Harmon allowed me the luxury of taking the summers off; Louis would cover for me.

Louis and his wife Charlotte worked with a summer theater in Ivoryton, Connecticut, a small town 40 miles northeast of New Haven and just up the road from Old Saybrook. Louis worked in the city during the week and joined his wife on the weekends.

The theater was built as an employee recreation hall and looked more like a barn than a theater. Perhaps that's why Charlotte referred to it as their "playhouse in a barn."

The Ivoryton Theater was one of the first self supporting theaters in America and had a parade of stars such as Marlon Brando, Ethel Waters, Tallulah Bankhead, Helen Hayes, Betty Grable and Groucho Marx.

We have to remember that in those days there was no air-conditioning and the New York theater district and most theaters would close down because of the heat. The ones that did stay open tried a pseudo air-conditioning scheme; they would fill the basement of the theater with blocks of ice and, by using fans with an elaborate duct system, cool air was blown into the theater. The lack of Broadway Theaters was filled by Summer Theaters in cooler sections of the country.

"Just what does a press agent do?" is a question that's often asked by curious and puzzled friends and acquaintances!

Usually, the press agent, or flack, starts working months in advance of rehearsals for the show he has been asked to publicize. The first announcement is often in the form of a release or an exclusive story placed in a theater's news column or trade paper. It tells of the acquisition of the play, "the property" in

Broadway jargon, by a producer, and when he intends it to open. If the producer has signed up with a particular theater for the Grand Opening, this is also mentioned.

This first announcement helps the producer raise the money for the show. The producer has plunked down option money, perhaps a thousand dollars, which gives him the rights to the play for a stated number of weeks or months. The intervening time gives him, or her, time to register the venture with the Securities and Exchange Commission, and to iron out other legal details.

The news release is the basic tool of the functioning flacker. Many of today's craftsmen are not trained journalists. In the '30's and 40's all publicists had to be able to compose an acceptable news story. The basic essential of how, what, where, and when was the norm, without a lot of extraneous adjectives or flowery sentences.

What with the shrinking newspaper market it is even more important that the press agent be terse so as to get his message into print or on the air. Many publicists, rather than release a news story to all the media, will first "leak" it to a news columnist, either by phone or in the form of a note detailing the basic information. The "leak" is followed up with a general release a week or so later that amplifies the original story with hard facts such as rehearsal dates, who is in the cast and what the show is about.

The telephone is a major tool of the publicist. When I first started in the business, if a press agent wanted to impress editors with the urgency and importance of the story, he would shoot off a long-worded Western Union Telegraph. It was an affective way of getting the editor's attention.

What is the difference between a theater press agent and a public relations consultant? Henry Sember, one of the gentlemen with whom I purchased the New York brownstone and who worked as New York Bell Telephone's PR man stated, "A press agent is paid to get his clients' names in the paper. A public relations man is paid to keep them out."

The ingenuity with which the publicist can keep the producer's upcoming production before the public's eye as 'news" is a test of how good the press agent does his job. For sheer volume of stories about a show that was to open, none has ever topped Billy Rose, producer of *Jumbo* by Rodgers and Hart, at the Hippodrome. The show encountered many delays since it combined elements of the circus with the Broadway Theater. With my mentor Richard Maney as chief press agent, each delay, and there were many of them, brought a wry comment from publicist Maney in the form of a creative release, which the papers printed. Drama critics looked forward to these gems from Maney and printed these bulletins on a by-weekly basis. *Jumbo* was a name that was well known by the time the show finally opened. The lengthy campaign was a lesson in how to make the best out of a sticky situation. And it took nothing more than a typewriter, a sense of humor and a creative press agent.

Timing is also essential for good publicity, and that sense some publicists have innately, particularly if they are regular readers of the daily tabloids. They know instinctively which issues are about to surface and which to stress. Some productions are luckier than others and can capitalize on the headlines of the day. Knowing when an editor or assignment chief has a deadline or when he can consider your "offering" is important. To badger a TV assignment editor late in the day, as he is trying to assemble his show for airing, can be fatal to the publicist. If the press agent catches the editor early in the day, before his crew is sent out, the agent is going to have a much better reception for his suggested feature.

The experienced publicist knows that "Variety's" deadline for a Wednesday publication is usually Monday, and that it is better if the story you're promoting can get into the works before then. Most news columns are set for specific days, although an important story can pop up on any day. But the usual announcement will get better consideration if it can be sent in at least 48 hours before the day it appears in the paper. Some stories are so hot that the flacker knows it will get published the next day if he gets to the editor early enough in the morning on the day before.

Timing was something that was important to me and for which I had great success. My girls can tell you that my Saturday mornings in New Hope were spent cranking out stories of the shows for which I was responsible. It was then off to the Post

Office to mail them before it closed. Using two different Post Offices in my area was important because I knew that one would guarantee me a New York delivery on Monday morning and the other was more reliable when it came to a Chicago delivery. Knowing the timing for when editors would receive my blurbs was a plus.

More wasted motion and goodwill is flushed down the drain by floundering agents than can be imagined. Being longwinded is one of the worst offenses. Editors are busy people. Too often memos, phone calls and releases are too long. If one or two sentences land in the paper, the publicist is fortunate. Advice; select the salient points, condense them and send that to the editors. It pays to take the time to condense all the news that will fit, and make it into a "punch" release. Remember George Bernard Shaw's apology for writing a letter instead of one of his cherished postal cards? "Please excuse the letter. I didn't have time to write a card."

A friendly editor once pointed out to me, at a metropolitan daily, that he kept an oversized wastebasket next to his desk. Grinning, he said, "I keep it handy for so-and–so's releases."

The theatrical publicist, unlike his higher paid colleague, the public relations counselor, has to sell tickets or he is out of work. He is paid only so long as the show runs; in other words, on a week-to-week basis.

The late Bob Sylvester, Broadway columnist, was a press agent for the Place Theater where the top vaudeville acts played, a different show every week. This was before he went to the Daily News and this is what he had to say about being a flack. He was teaching a course on "Becoming a Press Agent" to returning veterans of WWII. "Keep your eyes and ears open backstage. Get to know not only your performers but all the workers on the set, the wardrobe mistresses, stage managers, sound men and grips (the stage hands who move sets and props); get to know everyone. Stories they will tell you about what happens will make good copy."

The best definition of a professional in the theater was uttered by Don Walker, the Broadway musical arranger of such shows as *Fiddler on the Roof* and *Finian's Rainbow*. Don, who was a longtime Bucks County resident, and a graduate of the University of Pennsylvania's Wharton School, confided in me at pool side one day, "A pro is the person who sticks to his department." I couldn't agree with him more.

Theatrical publicity doesn't always go in the direction it is intended. Like any campaign, military or otherwise, its focus sometimes has to change. If the damage of the original isn't terminal, the flack must fit the conditions to the problem and make the proper revisions. One of the most famous publicity revisions on Broadway was the ad campaign of *Damn Yankees*.

*Damn Yankees* opened on Broadway at the 46th Street Theater during the spring of 1955. A musical comedy, it was based on Douglass Wallop's novel "The Year the Yankees Lost the Pennant." George Abbott directed the play and also helped Wallop write the script. Richard Adler and Gerry Ross were credited with the music and lyrics.

It was publicized by crafty Montreal-born, Rube Rabinovitch. The original publicity stressed the baseball aspect of the show and had Gwen Verdon, the lead actress, garbed in a baseball uniform. However, it didn't attract the number of customers Messrs. Bobby Griffith and Hal Prince intended, so the ad agency was called in to consult. It was decided it lacked sex appeal. A major change was made. Ms.Verdon, who possessed a stunning chassis, was garbed in scanty dance attire and posed with legs spread wide in an athletic stance. This new version played down the baseball background of the musical and accentuated the sexy dances and songs. When that hit the billboards it not only attracted customers to the theater but graffiti artists as well who, pen in hand, had a glorious time. No show had to replace its "paper" more often than *Damn Yankees*. A success at the box-office, it ran for 1,019 performances.

The work of a theatrical publicist certainly can be enhanced if he knows something about the business side of the theater. After all, it is his primary task, especially on tour, to be quite literally an advance agent. Many times the press agent came to town with a copy in hand of the contract for the show he was publicizing. This legal instrument stipulated how the house receipts were shared as well as the advertising terms. All of this had been negotiated in advance by his home office. Did his show have 70% of the receipts going to the producers, or only 65%? Did it stipulate that the theater would spend up to $ 2,000 a week on advertising and that everything above that had to be paid for by the theatrical event? Also, who would provide the stagehands and the musicians?

If the flack could sit down and help the company manager count up the night's receipts, he would have a better understanding of the success or failure of his show. "Count-up" meant first dividing the sold tickets from the unsold tickets and then entering the total dollars and cents of the sold tickets on the night's box office statements. These are printed forms that vary slightly from house to house but that are essentially the same. They are printed in multiple copies so that the theater, the show, the stars, and the playwright, all who get royalties, get copies.

Many veteran press agents used to be able to substitute for their company manager and officiate at the "count-up," which begins as soon as the curtain goes up. In the Shubert theaters in New York, it was a familiar sight to see a trusted, uniformed porter lugging the doorman's box, a heavy wooden affair where the orchestra and first and second balcony stubs were dropped into separate compartments. Each ticket office then sent around the unsold tickets. With Mr. Clancy, a slight, devoted Irishman who was house manager of the Broadhurst Theater, was the official for the count that would swing into action in an office atop the marquee. The stubs and the unsold tickets were laboriously counted by hand and entered on the statement sheet. This went on eight times a week. After the boxes were emptied, the porter would return them to the doorman to be ready for the next performance.

Not only was the statement important to the participants of the show but also to the U.S. government, which would take 10% as an amusement tax. To complicate things even further, in some cities the statement, verified and attested to by the treasurer and the company manager, had to be submitted to the municipal tax bureau.

It was necessary for the flack to have a symbiotic relationship with the company management, especially if he was on the road. When a press agent traveled on to the next stand from city to city, he had to depend on a reliable person to see that his actors kept their press and TV or radio appointments. Reminders to the actors were not enough. Sometimes the actors arrived in a particular city ahead of the show for rehearsals or whatever, which meant the press agent had to count on the company manager or stage manager to see that the star was delivered to the studio, awake and sober, for the press interview. In turn, the managers depended on the advance agent to provide hotel information and to reserve rooms for the cast. I remember well that this was a time-consuming job in some cities, particularly Washington and San Francisco where hotel space was limited.

The press agent is maligned frequently, never praised, yet indispensable in corralling, cajoling, and herding that necessary ingredient, the audience, into the theater. He or she is an important but unseen part of the professional theater team operating best in anonymity. Flacks are hardly hidden persuaders. It is just that they try to glamorize their stock-in-trade, the performers and creators, rather than themselves.

Are press agents necessary in the theater? Or is the saying "When you have a hit you don't need them, and when you have a flop it's their fault," correct?

Listen to what Brooks Atkinson, perhaps the best reviewer The New York Times ever fielded and, I might add, the only critic to have a theater named for him in New York has to say:

"Without a good battery of press agents along Broadway a drama editor would be without a good deal of valuable assistance. Press agents are not only a convenience in the assembling of news and pictures but the best of them are also good showmen and good writers."

Time magazine in the January, 1940 article titled "The Theater: Portrait of a Press Agent," summed it all up:

"No producer, tiny or tremendous, bucks Broadway without a press agent. He can't, because his union contract calls for one; but he couldn't anyway. A show without a press agent would be like a store without a show window."

# *Judy's Birthday party and The National Theater of Greece*

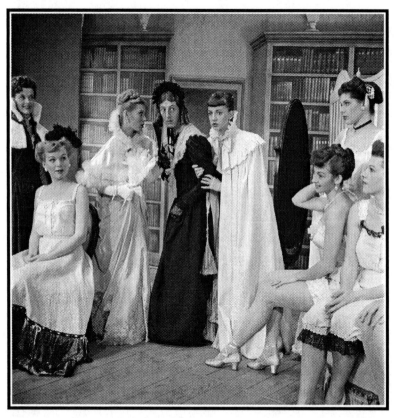

*Charley, (Ray Bolger) as his aunt, dressed in full Victorian regalia, surrounded by glorious ladies*

Sometimes a press agent can ask a favor of an actor and if you're lucky and the actor is friendly, he or she will honor your request. Ray Bolger, the "Scarecrow" of the *Wizard of Oz*, obliged.

We were trying out *Where's Charley*, a musical written by George Abbott and based on the play *Charley's Aunt* by Brandon Thomas. Lyrics and music were by Frank Loesser. It was in Philadelphia in the summer of 1948, and it just happened to be close to my daughter's 12$^{th}$ birthday. I reserved a box for the family and a few of Judy's girlfriends to see the show. At the end of the musical, the curtain fell, the actors took their bows, and the clapping subsided. Ray on his way offstage, looking directly at my daughter sitting in our box, said, "Happy birthday, Judy." Judy was delighted and I sat there with a huge grin on my face.

The show, also directed by George Abbott, opened in New York City to mixed reviews in the Fall of 1948 at the St. James Theater. However, due to a fluke, it managed to run for 792 performances. Ray Bolger was the catalyst that turned the show around due to a serious blunder on his part.

It seems that Mr. Bolger, playing the star role of Charley Wykeham, was about to sing the lead song, "Once in Love with Amy," when he unfortunately drew a blank and could not remember the words. An eight-year-old youngster was sitting on the second row. He had been listening to recordings of "Once in Love with Amy" for months and knew the words better than he did his own name. The kid on the second row threw Ray the words and saved the day.

The audience went wild, so much so that George Abbott decided to include the mistake in subsequent performances and let the audience sing along with Ray. For me, it was a blessing because it meant that instead of closing the show we could run it for almost two years.

In 1949, for his part as Charley, Ray Bolger won a Tony Award for the best actor in a musical play.

That I got involved with the National Theater of Greece was kind of a freak. I was working for Katharine Cornell, and her husband, Guthrie McClintic.

They established the Cornell Foundation which gave works of art to the Museum of Modern Art. They were very much into the arts and had a great admiration for the classics which led them to invite the National Theater of Greece to New York starring the famous Katina Paxinou and her husband, Alexis Minotis.

In those days there was no Olympic Airlines in which to dance in the aisles. Boat travel was all that was available and affordable, so everything came by boat, the scenery in one ship, and the actors in another. We planned to hold the shows at the Mark Hellinger Theater, then called the Warner. Not the most popular theater in New York but it did have space available. *My Fair Lady* hadn't opened there as yet, and it was a theater that wasn't used much.

In order to promote the plays, *Oedipus* and *Electra,* I had my partner Louis Harmon put up some pictures on the outside of the theater. The manager, Jimmy Troup, mistakenly thought that Louis was taking the pictures down and chased him down the block. Jimmy was quite embarrassed when he found out that it was his own union brother he was accusing.

One of the most disturbing things about the engagement was the lack of advanced ticket sales. No one bought tickets in advance of the opening. We thought, my god, we have a real turkey on our hands – all this money to get this Greek troupe over here and nobody is going to come to the theater. And if you didn't know it, the Mark Hellinger Theater was a large one with a lot of seats.

What I didn't know was that Stanley Gilkey, Mr. Mac's manager had a connection with the bishop of the Greek Orthodox Church, and Stanley had arranged with the "metropolitan of the area," (that's what the Bishop was known as) that he would pitch the plays from the pulpit in all the local churches.

I was dumbfounded on the day of the show. They started to line up and the line went clear around to 8th Avenue. Those Greeks weren't going to buy a penny's worth of tickets ahead of time. The show not only sold out, we had to extend the engagement.

Kelsey Allen was then the reviewer and ad salesman for *Women's Wear Daily*. He came to review the shows and, as was his custom, after hitting his seat he promptly fell asleep and started to snore. Of course, he probably felt that because the play was going to be in Greek, he wouldn't miss too much if he slept through the first act, for he knew no Greek. He also figured that if he slept through the first part certainly he'd be able to get the gist of the play after the intermission. There was only one problem. The Greeks were following their tradition; these plays have no intermission.

Kelsey woke up in time to see the curtain come down and walked out into the lobby and we conversed amiably. After fifteen minutes Kelsey went back into the theater, thinking he was going to see the second act. All of a sudden he came running out like somebody had lit a fire under his coat tails. "Where is everyone? What happened? Where did they go?"

Of course, without cracking a smile, we explained there was no intermission and what he witnessed was the end of the show and the audience had all gone home. Maybe next time he should stay awake if he wants to review a show?

The summer of 1951 was special. Both Babs and Judy referred to this sojourn the same way: "This was the trip that solidified our feeling that we were a family."

I had arranged to be away for more than three months and we made the best of it, touring Europe. I arranged with the Singer Motor Company of Coventry, England to supply us with one of their roadster touring cars. Knowing that at the end of our trip we would be shipping our Singer back home, I had the factory give us a left-hand drive rather than the standard English right-hand drive.

Our convertible, two-door roadster was waiting for us when the S.S. America docked in La Havre, France.

Our trip sounded like the song in *Kiss me Kate,* "The next stop Verona, da, dah, dah ...." Austria followed France, then on to Italy to see the sights in

Rome, Venice, and view the Leaning Tower of Pisa before heading off to Norway and Denmark. In Oslo we then boarded a ship bound for Scotland and from there drove down to London where we enjoyed a family reunion with the Goldmans and the Issacs who were visiting from South Africa.

Judy reminds me she celebrated her 15th birthday in Paris and spent many days in the Louvre with her mother. Nine year old Babs could endure just so many museums and preferred to feed the pigeons in ponds throughout our trip.

It was a most memorable trip for all of us and we were still talking to one another after being cooped up in our two-door Singer for all those months. And the Singer; it had a long life. After Judy turned 16, she drove herself and Babs to George School in it. It even distinguished itself by getting into show-biz. George School was putting on a play that needed the sound of a car. Judy was asked to drive the Singer up and down the George School driveway as the student audio persons recorded the sound.

*Scene* **3**

## *Our Greenwich Village Brownstone*

Because I was spending so much time on business during the week in New York, it seemed logical to me that an apartment of my own in the Big Apple would not be a luxury but a necessity. It also meant that Bobbie and the kids could join me on occasion from our home in New Hope, PA.

Being the cautious person that I am, I thought it prudent to rent first and see if having a New York apartment was really what we wanted to do. So, in 1953, we sublet a two bedroom at 34th Street and Lexington Avenue, a second floor walkup. Our six month trial proved more than satisfactory. Bobbie, with seventeen year old Judy and eleven year old Babs joined me in New York over the weekends and we enjoyed taking in the sights and the Broadway shows.

As fortune would have it, I found a brownstone in West Greenwich Village, which I purchased in

1954 with two other men, for $ 75,000. My share, $25,000. That was the same year I purchased our first Welsh Corgi.

While in her early teens, Babs was enamored with British Royalty and had scrapbooks to prove it. She was particularly fond of their Corgis, the breed of dog that young Queen Elizabeth favored. Besides making wonderful pets, the Pembroke Welsh Corgi is an excellent sheep herder that originated in Pembrokeshire, Wales.

I was working with *No Time for Sergeants* at the time and one of the members of the cast let me know that his pet dog, a Corgi, had just had a litter. Was I interested in buying one? "Yes," said I, thinking it might be a wonderful 12th birthday present for daughter Babs.

The following weekend, while Babs was visiting me in New York, we went to look at the litter of Corgis in the Village where the cast member lived and, of course, Babs, after playing with those cute little furry things, fell in love with them, and I'll have to admit, I was smitten too.

A month after our visit, but following her 12th birthday, I purchased one of the pups, placed it in a cardboard box, put the box in my car and proceeded to drive to my PA home. As I drove home I chuckled to myself at the vision of the surprised look on my daughter's face when she opened the box to find a Corgi puppy inside. All was going well until, four miles from home, I ran out of gas. What to do now? Certainly when the family brought the much needed gas so I could continue on my way, they would see the box in the back of the car and the surprise would be down the drain. They never noticed, and I was able to take the cardboard box out of the car and place it on the kitchen floor. Asking Babs to come into the kitchen, I had her open the box. Her face lit up and she was overcome with joy. "Why don't we name your puppy Dylan after Dylan Thomas?" I suggested. I explained to Babs that Dylan Thomas was a famous Welsh writer of poetry, short stories and scripts for film and radio. It seemed like an appropriate name for our new arrival. Babs agreed.

Dylan might have been the first Corgi to grace our home but certainly not the last. We owned a succession of Corgis lasting throughout our stay in New Hope.

John Willig, who worked for the New York Times as editor of the men's fashion department, took over the basement apartment of our newly purchased Brownstone.

We Jacobsons occupied the first floor which, with high ceilings and large rooms, was quite adequate for our family of four. However, when we purchased the property, our apartment was pretty much of a mess. The previous occupant had been a painter who had a lot of strange paintings on the walls which had to be removed and tossed. But our real problem was the bed bugs. Luckily, the exterminator rid us of these awful vermin. Bobbie had a friend who was an interior decorator and, with her help, they redid the apartment into a neat, attractive, pleasant place, with kitchen, a large sitting room, an alcove bedroom, and an adequate bathroom. We even had two fireplaces which worked.

Our third partner, Hank Sember, lived on the second floor; he had worked as a press agent for Orson Welles and the Mercury Theater and was currently with Bell Labs.

When we purchased the building, an elderly tenant, Mrs. Sato was living on the third floor in a lovely two-bedroom apartment and wanted to remain. We agreed to let her do so. As the years went by her $28.00 a month rent payment was but a mere pittance of what we should be charging. We attempted to raise her rent and asked her to vacate the premises if that was not acceptable. Unfortunately, it was an exercise in futility because she was grandfathered under the "rent control act." We realized the only way we were going to rid ourselves of Mrs. Sato was "feet first." And that's what happened, but many years later. After her death, Hank took over her apartment on the third floor.

Our brownstone was located at 67 Horatio Street, in the meat-packing district. It was hardly the glamorous place it is today. My girls remember, with disgust, walking from the bus or subway to our house and passing meat-packing plants with hides hanging outside, dripping with blood. It also didn't help that we were right across the street from a large meat packer who insisted on running large, noisy trucks in and out at three and four in the morning.

But, for convenience it was perfect for me and my work in the theater. When not on the road, my schedule followed a pattern; I would go to New York Monday morning, come back Wednesday after the matinee, then return to New York Thursday morning only to leave again for home on Friday afternoon.

Before boarding the Friday train, I would buy as many New York papers as I could handle, so I could read about what was happening on Broadway over the weekend. Also tucked under my arm was the early edition of The New York Times Sunday Art section which Brooks Atkinson's secretary, Clara Rotter, procured and saved for me.

Taking the subway to the bottom of Manhattan, I boarded the ferry which took me across the Hudson River to the Jersey City Terminal where The Crusader was waiting to take me home.

I always looked forward to the ferry ride across the Hudson. The fresh air, the view of the city, the splashing water as we rushed across was always invigorating and a nice change from the routine of the day.

Although the Reading Railroad was much more interested in moving millions of tons of anthracite coal on its railways than people, thank goodness they did provide one passenger train. The Crusader was a plush, streamlined, stainless steel, five-car train and a deluxe way to travel.

I would hop on The Crusader and ride to the Hopewell Station, getting back to New Hope for a relaxed Friday night dinner. As a creature of habit, I, on arriving home would have a cocktail with Bobbie, which gave us time to catch up, and then have dinner, but not before 7:00. To have it earlier, I felt, was barbaric.

When Babs left for college in 1960, Bobbie and I moved to the New York apartment during the week and returned to New Hope on the weekends. It was a nice switch, giving us more time together now that we didn't have the responsibility of our youngest at home. What's the expression? Life begins when the kids leave home and the dog dies? Well, the kids left but thank God the dog didn't die. Oh well.

During the almost forty years that we owned our West Greenwich Village home, we saw huge changes take place. What was once a middle-class working neighborhood filled with meat packing houses slowly morphed and was re-gentrified to compete with its wealthy first cousin, East Greenwich Village.

In the late 90's, our New York house sold for three million dollars which was split three ways. Not bad for my investment of only $25,000.

*Scene* **4**

# Look Back in Anger and the Entertainer

Lewis Harmon and I had been hired by David Merrick as his publicists for *Look Back in Anger,* a John Osborne play that opened on Broadway in 1956. It had been a huge success in England both artistically and commercially. The play gave its name to a whole movement, "The Angry Young Men." These were a group of middle-class playwrights and novelists who were disillusioned with traditional English society and wrote about it. *Look Back in Anger* was misunderstood in the United States, never getting a real foothold.

One night, as *Look Back in Anger* entered its second act, a woman sitting in the audience, jumped onto the stage and slapped its leading man, Kenneth Haigh on the cheek while his co-players, Alan Bates and Mary Ure, looked on in astonishment. The woman was subsequently hustled off stage and the show continued.

At the time, Lewis and I were not in the audience. We were handling opening night procedures for Arthur Miller's *The Crucible,* in an Off-Broadway theater on 33$^{rd}$ Street. But, we had given the back stage manager of *Look Back in Anger* our phone number and told him that if anything out of the ordinary happened he was to call us immediately.

Following the incident, the manager called and, realizing it would make good press, I dialed my AP drama-editor friend, William H. Glover, Jr., at his home, to tell him what had gone on in the theater. Bill called his city desk and within minutes the "slapping of our lead by a strange woman" had made the papers and the airwaves.

It isn't often that a publicist gets caught in a charade brought on by a client, but it does happen. We who were nurtured by the "Master," Maney, believed that reliability and truth were the two most valuable assets a publicist could possess. Our reputation was built on those values.

I learned, only too soon, that the incident was a hoax, designed by Producer David Merrick as a publicity stunt. To my chagrin, I found out that David preferred trickery to honesty anytime, anywhere and, at times, he would deceive his own staff. Obviously, it had worked with Lewis and me. Nor was this to be his last act of deceiving the public. Merrick took out a full-page ad with phony raves from New Yorkers, whom he paid, with the same names as the reviewers. That's deception to the fullest.

Was the show faltering, as David later contended? A look at the box office gross would have indicated no, either before or after his "cute" stunt. That was David; facts didn't matter; just get the name of the show mentioned. He was P.T. Barnum come to life.

But, you know, Broadway isn't a circus!

What was his legacy? Chiefly it was in reassessing the way shows were advertised and then allotting more of the budget and weekly operating overhead to that advertising. Before Merrick, ads were small, consisting chiefly of one-or two-column affairs and with little or no art work. Merrick changed all that.

His tragedy was that he began to believe his own stunts. His persona as the meanest, sharpest guy who could best anyone he dealt with, took root. Deviousness became his way of life. He even trained his eyebrows to look devilish a la Al Hirschfeld and became a walking caricature. He didn't have ulcers; he gave them.

My most vivid memory was the sighting of Merrick in Shubert Alley as one of his fellow-producers, Arthur Cantor, stood guard at the Booth Theater's stage door. A memorial service was about to begin for the theater's general manager, Jack Schlissel.

"David, you are not welcome here," Cantor said.

It was a fitting epitaph for Merrick.

My last official contact with Merrick was also memorable.

*The Entertainer*, written by John Osborne, opened in London at the Royal Court Theater on

April 10<sup>th</sup>, 1957. It arrived in New York in 1958 through the efforts of David Merrick. I was hired to publicize *The Entertainer* which had as its star, Laurence Olivier, for whom the play had been written. Olivier played the part of Archie Rice, a washed up music hall comedian.

Arrangements were made to bring Mr. Olivier, along with his entire cast, to American shores. To make it easier for everyone, this was to be accomplished on a weekend. David told me to set up an interview for Olivier and interested parties such as the New York drama editors and reporters.

Problem: Laurence Olivier hated to be interviewed but was persuaded to give us one shot if I set it up correctly. I picked the ballroom of the Algonquin Hotel where enough chairs were provided to handle the multitude that was sure to come. The scene was set for the famous English actor's arrival.

David and I were at the airport in plenty of time to meet the arriving entourage. All seemed to be on schedule. Two planes were used because Olivier refused to travel with Brenda De Banzie, who portrayed his wife in the play. The first plane arrived without incident but the second, Olivier's plane, was detoured to Baltimore due to bad weather.

What to do? The interview was all set up, but our star subject was stuck at the airport in Baltimore.

Thank goodness for my old friend, Lew Azrael. I got him on the phone in Baltimore, told him of the situation, and asked him to call the reporter who was covering the airport. Could the reporter please shepherd Olivier from the airport to the train station and supply him with enough American money for his train ticket.

It worked, and the interview did take place on schedule.

On the front row was Sam Zolotow, an obnoxious drama critic from the *New York Times*, who distinguished himself by heckling anybody he could.

"Mr Olivier," he asked, "What is the purpose of this meeting?"

Olivier: "To make David Merrick and Sol Jacobson happy."

*The Entertainer* played to mixed reviews but lasted week after week due to the presence of Olivier. Larry, who would not answer to any other appellation even though he had been knighted by the Queen, had the habit of never getting to the theater early. As the last of the audience were taking their seats, I watched "Sir Laurence" come running down the street, ducking into the stage door just in time. He'd slap on his makeup and on stage he'd go. He wished to spend as little time as possible with his co-actor, Brenda De Banzie. She had an interest in him beyond the stage while his interests were in Joan Plowright, who was acting in *The Taste of Honey.* They were later married.

*Sir Lawrence Olivier as "The Entertainer"*

Meanwhile back in New Hope in the late 1950's our girls were growing up. Judy had graduated from George School, and Babs was a day student there.

Blythe Danner was a George School classmate of Babs and a frequent visitor in our New Hope home. Babs and Blythe have remained good friends throughout the years and when Blythe heard from Babs that a book was being written about one of her favorite people - that would be me - she wanted to be included.

# The following is Blythe's contribution:

I will try to be succinct in my memories of Sol and the Jacobsons but could wax poetic about them all day. They changed my life! When Babs and I were at George School together we were 'Day Students'. She has been my best friend since those early teenage years. The Day Students were a bit like the 5th wheel at G.S. The boarders were considered the 'cool' kids for the most part. They were, a lot of them from NYC and quite sophisticated next to us country bumpkins. Heller Halliday, Mary Martin's daughter was in our class as was Patty Hammerstein, Oscar's granddaughter. It seemed to be a haven for showbiz kids. Keir Dullea, with whom I later worked on B'way, had graduated just before I arrived as a freshman, George Segal had been there before that, and to me the most impressive alumn of all was Stephen Sondheim, who was there long before us. (Ten years ago I had the thrill of playing Phyllis in the B'way revival of FOLLIES) And I soon discovered Babs was no country bumpkin. When I visited her at home I found her family to be the most fascinating of them all. They were Quakers and addressed one another as 'thee' instead of 'you'. Bobbie, Bab's mother read Chekhov to us while she reclined in a hammock in the garden of the house on Windy Bush Rd. in New Hope while Mozart wafted out in the air as records played inside on the stereo. They took me with them to outdoor chamber concerts in the summer and to my first Chekhov play, the SEAGULL at the Bucks County Playhouse. I couldn't leave my seat after the curtain came down, so deeply moved was I by the glorious Rosemary Harris's performance as Nina. (Little did I know that I would work with her 15 years later in the NEW YORK IDEA at BAM, also would be directed by Ellis Raab, then her husband, in TWELFTH NIGHT and THE PHILADLPHIA STORY years later. He had directed this SEAGULL and his company, APA, was in residence in Bucks Co. I would later work with several members of the company who were on stage that day.) That experience was truly life changing. The passion, humor, heartbreak and beauty of Chekhov and Rosemary's performance hit me like a lightning bolt. I had to be a part of this. To this day playing NIna at the Williamstown Theatre Festival a little more than a decade later is the memory I cherish the most in my career. And I pay tribute to and thank Sol, Bobbie and Babs from the bottom of my heart for that introduction to the great master. Perhaps I'd never have known the depth of the beauty of Anton C. if I hadn't first experienced it with those extraordinary people.

Sol, was such a lovely man, erudite but quietly so. Everyone says he was an unusual pressman in that he was such a gentleman, not in the least bit pushy or overpowering. He was soft spoken. I often wondered how he accomplished so much as a successful pr guy. I guess he "walked softly and carried a big stick.!" The love for his wife and family was palpable. There was a serenity and quiet happiness that resonated throughout that house. For me it was a sanctuary. Every chance I got I'd race up to New Hope from my home in Richboro in my little Saab and always be welcomed with open arms. Bobbie taught me how to crewel embroider and was often covered in flour from whipping up her delicious soufflés and cookies. I adored her, as I did Sol. They always made me feel very complete and comfortable.

I saw the shows Sol was working on back then: FIORELLO, which I loved and my favorite, SHE LOVES ME. The record played constantly at home after my children were born and we all knew every lyric of every song. When I was an exchange student in Berlin in 1960-61 ( the year the wall was built) I received in the mail from Sol an L.P. of TENDERLOIN which had just opened on B'way. I loved it and played it day and night. A funny aside is, my future sister-in-law, Dottie Frank, now Danner, was in the show though she wasn't to meet my brother until years later. Sol was very generous in other ways too, in that Babs and I often stayed in his Greenwich Village apt and saw a variety of shows. I don't know how many times we were in 'standing room only' for WESTSIDE STORY, another early passion. No production that I've seen since has ever come close to the raw emotion and dazzle that that production had. I sometimes wonder what would have happened if the Jacobsons hadn't been in my life. For me they were the extraordinary teachers most people recall when asked who influenced them the most in their early lives. Certainly my beautiful parents with their dazzling soprano and tenor voices and love and care had a tremendous impact but the Jacobsons introduced me to a gravitas, spiritual sensibility and love of serious art I'd never known before. I'm forever indebted to Sol, Bobbie and Babs for a giving me a richness of experience that I cherish to this day and will continue to until my last day!!

*Scene* **5**

*West Side Story*

*In a modern day Romeo and Juliet story, Larry Kert,
as Romeo, woos Carol Lawrence, his Juliet*

*West Side Story* opened in New York on September 26th, 1957 at the Winter Garden Theater to mixed reviews.

Jonathan Cott's interview with Leonard Bernstein in 1990 for *Rolling Stones* Magazine gives us some insight into why the reviews were mixed:

> "Everyone told us that *West Side Story* was an impossible project ... And we were told no one was going to be able to sing augmented fourths, as with "Ma-ri-a" ... Also, they said the score was too rangy for pop music ... Besides, who wanted to see a show in which the first-act curtain comes down on two dead bodies lying on the stage?... And then we had the really tough problem of casting it, because the characters had to be able not only to sing but dance and act and be taken for teenagers. Ultimately, some of the cast were teenagers, some were 21, some were 30 but looked 16. Some were wonderful singers but couldn't dance very well, or vice versa ... and if they could do both, they couldn't act."

It was not a hit, so management decided to send it south to Washington, DC to see if it would get any traction there. After a short stay in Washington, DC, where once again the reviews were mixed, back it came to New York. I was hired by Bobby Griffith and Hal Prince, the producers of the show, to be the press agent. But, there was a caveat. I had to come up with an idea that would guarantee that Brooks Atkinson, the famous *New York Times* reviewer of

Broadway shows, and others would change their minds and write something more positive this time.

I suggested, "Why not have Lenny (Leonard Bernstein who wrote the score for the show,) direct the orchestra on opening night?" I knew Lenny when he was a kid studying at the Curtis Institute in Philadelphia. I remember at one meeting I asked him why he came to Curtis to study, being a New Englander. His answer was typically Lenny. "Why? Curtis offered me a full scholarship. It was four years of free study; besides, Curtis was known to be an excellent school for what I was studying"

My gut told me that if Lenny directed the orchestra, playing his own songs on opening night, *West Side Story* would be on its way to being one of the greatest musicals of Broadway. Although Lenny was the busy musical director of the New York Philharmonic, he did conduct on opening night, and the rest is history.

Jerome Robbins, as choreographer and director of the show, was one of the few geniuses I've had the pleasure of working for. When first approached to take the job as choreographer, he was reluctant to take the position. He found the dance routines too demanding and the musical score difficult to interpret. But he finally did accept with the stipulation that rehearsals of the dance scenes had to be eight weeks rather than the usual four.

In *West Side Story* he revolutionized the Broadway musical by introducing impossible dance routines that only youngsters could endure. So strenuous, in fact, were the dances that a doctor was always on call.

*One of the many difficult dance scenes*

One of Jerry's creative innovations; the Sharks and the Jets, were not allowed to rehearse their routines together. Jerry hired two separate theaters for rehearsals, feeling that there would be greater spontaneity in dislike for each other's gang if they were separated before going on stage. It worked. The fight scene between the Sharks and the Jets still stands as one of the classic scenes in musical theater.

*The Sharks and the Jets rumble*

Jerome Robbins, Leonard Bernstein and Arthur Laurents (who wrote the book), conceived the idea in 1951 of writing a musical based on William Shakespeare's *Romeo and Juliet*. However, the protagonists were not the Sharks, a gang of first generation Americans from Puerto Rico, against the Jets, a gang of white Americans. Their gangs were to be Jews and Italian Catholics and the story line had a Jewish boy falling in love with an Italian Catholic girl. The name of the show was to be *East Side Story*.

Due to the trio's heavy commitments, the idea was shelved for six years and, when they finally started working on the play in earnest, the Jewish/Italian Catholic idea had lost its social relevancy. The middle fifties, unfortunately, saw a great struggle between the new immigrants of Puerto Rico and the established white gangs. It was this social unrest that the trio used as a background for their musical. And so *West Side Story* was born in its present form.

*Stephen Sondheim, Arthur Laurents, Hal Prince, Bobby Griffith (seated), Leonard Bernstein and Jerome Robbins*

Leonard Bernstein composed the music but had no interest in writing the lyrics. He turned to a relatively unknown lyricist, Stephen Sondheim, who was referred to him by the show's producer, Harold Prince. It would be Stephen Sondheim's debut on Broadway.

Although unknown, Stephen had traveled in musical circles and was no stranger to the American musical theater. As a youngster, while at George School, a Pennsylvania Quaker prep school outside Newtown, in Bucks County, PA, he wrote a musical called "By George."

Stephen was an only child from a dysfunctional family and preferred to spend his time away from George School with his classmate and friend, Jimmy Hammerstein, at the Hammersteins' home in Doylestown, PA., rather than go home. It was here at the knee of the great Oscar Hammerstein II that he was encouraged to write words to music. It was also here that Stephen found a surrogate father. Oscar schlepped him to many of his shows in New York and it was at the opening of *South Pacific* in 1949 that Stephen met Harold Prince, the same Harold Prince that had recommended him to Leonard Bernstein as the lyricist for *West Side Story* eight years later.

A cute story, whether apocryphal or not, is worth noting: During one visit, Stephen asked Oscar if he would review *By George,* not telling him it was his creation. "It's the worst thing I have ever seen," was Oscar's comment. "However, if you want to know why it's terrible, I'll tell you." Oscar then proceeded, for the rest of the afternoon, to analyze the play. Stephen's comment, "In that afternoon I learned more about songwriting and the musical theater than most people learn in a lifetime"

And believe it or not, when Stephen was approached to be the lyricist of *West Side Story*, he was lukewarm in accepting the job. He had read the script and found it depressing. It was Hammerstein senior who urged him to accept, saying "It will be good experience for you." That's an understatement if ever I heard one. *West Side Story* launched Stephen Sondheim into a remarkable career in the musical theater as a lyricist and song- writer with shows like: *Gypsy, Company, A Funny Thing Happened on the Way to the Forum,* and *Sweeney Todd*, to mention just a few.

To celebrate opening night we had a party at Roseland on 52[th] Street with the cast and the backers. We all felt we had a hit and the notices agreed with even Brooks Atkinson changing his mind.

The latest revision of *West Side Story* opened on Broadway at the Palace Theater, on February 23, 2009 and was well received. The play bill gave credit to Jerome Robbins as the director and choreographer of the original production and noted "the choreography reproduced" by Joey McKneely. But even more delightful was Arthur Laurents, now in his nineties, who wrote the book, directed this revision and introduced an exciting innovation.

Maria, played by Josefina Scaglione who hails from Argentina and Anita, Maria's girlfriend, played by Karen Olivo, were both of Latin descent.

When the Puerto Rican actors were on stage speaking to each other, they spoke in Spanish. The two languages, English and Spanish, clashing on stage only added to the excitement of this famous musical.

*Carol Taylor cuts the birthday cake celebrating the third year of West Side Story backstage at the Winter Garden Theater with fellow players, George Marcy, Pat Birch, Alan Johnson, Allyn Ann McLearie and Don Grilley looking on.*

*The Leonard Bernstein musical enters its fourth year as one of Broadway's resigning hits.*

## *Fiorello, Take Her, She's Mine and A Funny Thing Happened on the Way to the Forum*

In the Fall of 1959, Louis and I found ourselves extremely busy and thought that now was the time to look for an associate to help with the load. It would also allow us to take on up to six shows at one time. Mary Elizabeth Bryant got the job.

It was through a fluke that I hired Mary Bryant in the first place. In retrospect, Mary's employment sounds more like fiction than one of reality but sometimes the true story is stranger than fiction. Unanswered questions; how did Mary know we were looking for someone and who told her to call me?

Here's the strange story:

My wife's mother, Jessalyne Scott engaged an African American maid who served her well for 35 years. When my mother-in-law died, Mary Bryant retired to her home town of Raleigh, NC.

One day I came into the office to find a note that Mary Bryant visited and left a phone number so that I could contact her. Mary wished to set up an appointment; she was interested in employment. I dialed the number, heard the familiar southern drawl in her voice and we arranged to meet in a few days. I believed that I would be seeing Mary Bryant of Raleigh, NC, my mother-in-law's maid.

You can imagine my amazement when a Caucasian woman with an Alabama accent, whom I had known as an actress at Hedgerow, walked into my office for her scheduled interview, introducing herself as Mary Bryant. I had forgotten that there were two Mary Bryants with southern accents.

Mary was hired although she had no prior experience in our field, but I believed that with training she would make an adequate press agent. Ultimately, she became my associate.

I later learned that Mary had not called me out of the blue. Rather it was her intimate friend, George Abbott, who suggested she call.

Mary's début as a press agent on Broadway began with *Fiorello*. She couldn't have picked a better musical to start her career.

The musical *Fiorello* is the story of New York City's Mayor, a Republican reformer who took on the corrupt Democratic machine known as Tammany Hall. Music was by Jerry Bock with lyrics by Sheldon Harnick. George Abbott not only directed the show but helped Jerome Weidman write the book which was drawn from the 1955 story, *Life with Fiorello* by Ernest Cuneo.

*Fiorello* opened at The Broadhurst Theater on November 23, 1959, moved to The Broadway Theater in May of that year and closed after 795 performances in October of 1961. To say it was a hit from the start is an understatement. It kept our office busy for almost two years.

Brooks Atkinson's review in the New York Times under the title, "Little Flower Blooms Again" says it all;

> "It is exciting; it is enjoyable and it is decent ... Jerry Bock has set ... a bouncy score ... As the writer of lyrics, Sheldon Harnick is in an unfailingly humorous frame of mind ... Under Mr. Abbott's invincible stage direction, the whole show comes alive with gusto ...The cast could not be more winning or in better voice."

As was George Abbott's custom, we met the morning after opening night to discuss the play and hear about George's next play. During the meeting I made the comment that *Fiorello* was such an extraordinary and provocative play that it would win a Pulitzer Prize. I was pooh-poohed by those gathered. In 1960 *Fiorello* won The Pulitzer Prize for drama.

Joseph Pulitzer was a successful publisher who founded The *St Louis Post-Dispatch* and purchased the *New York World*. Upon his death in 1911, Columbia University found themselves recipients of a large bequest thanks to Pulitzer's will. A portion of the largess was used to establish the University's

School of Journalism in 1912 and, five years later, the Pulitzer Prize. The prizes, in twenty-one categories, are awarded in April of every year.

Tom Bosley who played the lead in Fiorello as the Mayor earned a "Tony Award for Best Performance by a Featured Actor in a Musical." Tom was a well known actor from his role as Howard Cunningham in the ABC sitcom, *Happy Days* and was a pleasure to work with.

*Mrs. Maria LaGuardia tips Tom Bosley's hat, as Hal Prince and "The Little Flower" look on*

The comedy *Take Her, She's Mine* ran for a year on Broadway opening in late December of 1961, produced by Harold Prince, directed by George Abbott and with Carl Fisher as the general manager. The show was written by Phoebe and

Henry Ephron. It was star studded, with Art Carney, Richard Jordon and Elizabeth Ashley.

Art Carney distinguished himself by scaring the hell out of me. He would never tell me where he was staying. To say the least, this is not helpful to a press agent. How can you set up an interview or a photo shoot if you don't know how to get in touch with your client? That being said, in spite of this idiosyncrasy, he never missed an engagement.

When you are on the road with a play it isn't often that one of the main actors is canned and another hired. But that is exactly what happened in *Take Her, She's Mine.* Hank Whittemore, the youngster who played the part of Alex Loomis, was dismissed and Richard Jordon took his place. It was Richard's debut on Broadway and the beginning of a successful acting career on stage and screen.

The problems these changes cause the press agent are many. All of the advertising has to be reworked quickly, letting the public know that Richard Jordon is now playing the part of Alex Loomis. This we accomplished but, of course it does not address how Hank Whittemore must have felt about being dumped. I often wondered how it happened and it wasn't until years later, in reading Hank's memoirs that I found out.

It was through the good offices of The Deborah Coleman Agency, that Hank, at the age of twenty, obtained an audition for *Take Her, She's Mine.* All went well and he even remembered hearing George Abbott and Hal Prince laughing in the back of the darkened theater as he read his lines. After a number of call backs, Hank got the job playing Alex Loomis. Rehearsals started in the early Fall and all seemed to be going well. It was during the rehearsal of Act 2 that the problem began. Hank was playing the part of the fiancé of Frank Michaelson's daughter, played by Elisabeth Ashley. I quote from his memoir:

> "The scene was a pizza parlor with Carney, the father; Ashley, the daughter, working there as a waitress; and me, the fiancé. I had a line to say and Carney was to ask her, "What's so funny?" But every time I said my line, Ashley stared back stone-faced until Carney shouted to director George Abbott, *'How can I say my line unless she smiles?'* At which point Liz turned to me and snapped, "Well, make it funny!" That was it. Producer Hal Prince called a break and bounded up on stage to tell me they were giving me two weeks' pay. 'She has a run-of-the-play contract,' he said, referring to Ashley, 'so obviously we have to let you go.'"

*Take Her She's Mine* was the last show in which Mary Bryant was my associate. She must have learned enough from us and needed to get out on her own. And so she set up her own agency.

In the spring of 1962 *A Funny Thing Happened on the Way to the Forum* was launched in New Haven, Connecticut for a three day trial. George Abbott was director and Hal Prince, producer. I was their press agent.

The musical comedy, *Forum* all started around Yale University's swimming pool, where the "Yale

Dramats," an undergraduate acting group, performed it for their director Bert Shevelove. Shevelove had written the play along with his partner Larry (Mash) Gelbert, and Stephen Sondheim added the music and lyrics. The show was based on the farces of Plautus, that bawdy ancient Roman author who had long been a source of burlesque sketches.

The story line was simple. It told the tale of a Roman slave named Pseudolus who attempts to win his freedom by helping his young master woo the girl next door. That's funny just thinking about it; add Zero Mostel as Pseudolus and it is even funnier.

However, the first night audience didn't know what to make of the show. When David Burns, a favorite comedian, on the order of W.C. Fields, stepped through the curtain dressed in his toga and sang Sondheim's "Love Is In The Air" the ticketholders were mystified by the opening number which was supposed to introduce and explain the play. In New Haven, *Forum* got off to a very bad start.

After our three day run we moved to Washington DC where we were booked for two weeks. Advance sales were not strong, and word-of-mouth not encouraging. Again the audience sat befuddled at opening night. The next day the three daily newspapers were non-committal but the reviewers expressed the hope that George Abbott, using his magical expertise, could reshape the show in some way and make it a hit. It looked like we had a flop on our hands. The audience just didn't get the gist of the play and the ticket sales proved it. During our weeks in Washington we had one of the National Theater's worst gross receipts in their history.

Happily, "Mr. A.," the dean of Broadway's stagers, heeded what the newspaper critics had written and called a special production meeting.

"Stephen", Abbott told composer-lyricist Sondheim, "you have to let the audience know what this show is all about. Write another opening number."

Believe it or not, within days, Stephen came up with his dazzling, brilliant, stage-storming opening song "Comedy Tonight."

When Abbott and Prince heard the new song this was the conversation that followed:

"This is just right, just fine Stephen," said Abbott. "Now Hal," he said turning to Prince, "grab Jerry Robbins and get him started reworking this opening number. I know he's here in town because he is in Washington to receive a Kennedy Award. Tell him I'll give him a percentage of the director's royalties if he'll stage this number. I am convinced it will take a choreographer like Jerry to make it work."

Prince moved with alacrity. That night after watching the show, Jerry agreed to help and wanted no program credit but he did insist that the New York opening be postponed for three days, to give him enough time to re-work the dance routines. It was my job to tell the public there would be a three day delay.

*A Funny Thing Happened on the Way to the Forum* finally made its appearance on Broadway on May 8, 1962 at the Alvin Theater. It went on to run for 964 performances and then spawned duplicates on the road and in London as well as two later revivals on Broadway. It was a Cinderella story that came true.

*George Abbott and Hal Prince, on the phone opening night,*
*waiting to hear the critics' review of A Funny Thing*
*Happened on the Way to the Forum*

Stephen Sondheim's rewrite of the opening number did the trick and was true genius. How many people could come up with a new number so quickly? And a hit song to boot!

In all my years on Broadway, I don't know of any other show that was saved by a single song.

*Scene* **7**

# *Dawson City and Foxy*

*Place Grand Theatre in Dawson City*
*Bea Lillie, aka Lady Peel, is in the middle*

*My preferred photographer and dear friend*

*Eileen Darby*

I've found myself waking up in remote spots like London and Ontario rather than the more conventional try-out towns of New Haven, Boston and Philadelphia but talk about remoteness; none can compare with Dawson City, Yukon. This is where, on July 1, 1962, we tried out the musical *Foxy* starring that incomparable clown, Bert Lahr. Why mount a full-blown Broadway musical comedy in such an out-of-the way location as Dawson City, some 4,500 miles from Times Square? It was all the mad-dog notion of that Canadian pintsized Barnum, Tom Patterson.

Tom, who dreamed up the Stratford Shakespeare Festival to invigorate his native Ontario village of Stratford, had been looking around for a way to pry some more dollars loose from Ottawa for another theatrical venture in the Dominion.

A wary Diefenbaker Conservative government took a lot of special lobbying. But Tom was persistent and persuasive. Eventually he, with the help of some other Canadians, convinced the Northern Affairs tourist section that it ought to rebuild Arizona

Charley's Palace Grand Theatre in Dawson City, a dance hall of bandbox proportions that possessed a stage where traveling theater companies entertained the gold-prospector "sourdoughs" and their girl friend "doxies" during the 1897-98 gold rush. In fact, the enterprise that Tom wanted to father he entitled *The Gold Rush Festival.*

Tom persuaded Broadway's Robert Whitehead, a fellow Canadian, to serve as producer of a show that would relight the Palace Grand. It was Whitehead who conceived the idea of transforming *Volpone*, the old Ben Jonson comedy classic about lust and greed, into a memorial to the intrepid seekers of gold nuggets along the Yukon and called it *Foxy.* "Volpone" means "the fox."

Ring Lardner, Jr., and Ian McLelland Hunter were employed to rewrite the book that transferred the action from Medieval Italy to the turn-of-the-century Canadian Arctic. Bobby Dolan and Johnny

Mercer signed on to do the music and lyrics. I got involved through Bob's manager, Stanley Gilkey, for whom I had worked before. Stanley was also to shepherd the company to their northern post.

Ever since I was a youngster it had been my ambition to trek to one of the Poles, North or South. I didn't care which. While this wasn't exactly the North Pole, at least it was up in that direction.

When Bert Lahr consented to go, neither Bob Whitehead nor manager Gilkey or director Bobby Lewis realized what they were in for. They had engaged an actor who was so deathly afraid of flying and planes that he wrote it into his contract; he would never have to get into an airplane on any condition.

So, now the question was how to move a full scale musical comedy troupe to the Yukon without resorting to the air. Time was running out. The Festival was set to open July 1 and run through August 17.

Fortunately, Whitehead and Patterson proved to be logistical geniuses. They moved the company across the continent by rail, Canadian rail, of course. They rehearsed all the way, to the astonishment and consternation of their fellow passengers. Rehearsals continued at the provincial performing arts center in British Columbia, and then on to the Queen Elizabeth Theater in Vancouver. There they awaited the arrival of the Canadian Pacific coastal steamer, which sailed, on a weekly schedule from Seattle to Skagway, Alaska, a five-day junket which, during the month of June, was fully booked.

The full booking didn't seem to faze the pow-
ers- that-be in Ottawa. They preempted the
necessary staterooms, to the disgust of numerous
tourists who had booked passage months before.

As the Canadian Pacific steamer pulled its way
into a small port on the Inner Passage, Bobby Dolan
and Bert Lahr were lolling on the deck at the railing
when they spotted some youngsters on the beach.
"They're Eskimos," exclaimed the star. "No, Bert,"
answered the composer, "those are Indians." As the
vessel hove to, Bobby thought to ask the kids.
"What are you?" he shouted. They looked startled.
"What do you mean what are we, we're Indians."
Bobby turned to Bert. "See?" The Angry Lion
snarled, "Kids. What do they know?"

Once in Skagway it was over the Chilkoot Pass
thanks to the services of the Whitehorse & Yukon
Railroad, a famed narrow-gauge system.

The journey was a tedious one for the company;
consider that they could have flown, with changes at
Edmonton or Vancouver, in less than 24 hours, as I
did later. Bert had acquired an expensive all-bands,
shortwave, portable radio to keep abreast of the
world that summer. As the train hurtled westward,
he kept playing with the set when he wasn't being
called for rehearsals in the club car. "Hark!..Shush!"
he commanded his cohorts at the dinner table. "I've
just pulled in Moscow." Indeed he had. It was
Moscow all right, but Moscow, Idaho.

From Whitehorse it was another 350 mile trip
by a dusty road along the Yukon on a chartered bus

to the final destination, Dawson City. The troupe arrived a scant week ahead of opening night.

Never was a troupe of outsiders more warmly welcomed by the excited band of Dawson City residents, many of whom lodged the players and musicians in their frame residences on those picture-book hills nestled under Midnight Dome with its surrounding mountains.

Of course the story of the hegira, the Lahrs' trip to Dawson, was great copy to the press agent. I relayed the whole saga to Artie Gelb, then assistant city editor of the *New York Times*. He was delighted with my story and assigned a feature writer and cartographer to detail the roundabout route of the Foxy Company to their tryout lair. The show, you see, was planned for Broadway. A pre-Broadway tryout, so help me. That was the billing.

What amused Gelb was his sharp memory of Bert Lahr as Rusty Krause, a daredevil ace in some aerial sequences in the film version of *Flying High*. It had been shot six inches off the ground in a Hollywood studio, with trick effects. The thought of Lahr, the Cowardly Lion of *Wizard of Oz* fame, shunning planes and traveling all that way on the train, was irresistible.

The feature broke, complete with maps of the convoluted route, and was a sendoff for the entire enterprise. It was picked up by the *Times*, syndicated and broke well, especially in Canada and the West Coast.

But to our dismay, all that wonderful publicity had little effect at the box-office. There had been a landslide on the Alcon Highway at Tok Junction that Spring. Traffic had to detour miles around Dawson City, isolated as if it had the plague by the mishap. If you really needed to get to Dawson City it was necessary to take an involved detour that included fording the Yukon River, all thanks to the Tok mud slide. And when you got there, there were no Hiltons and no Sheratons on hand; just scant accommodations in tourist homes.

I'll always be grateful to *Foxy* for two happenings: getting to know a little of the Yukon and Alaska, and Glenna Syse, the Chicago *Sun Times'* delightful and bright theater reviewer. She is a concocter of some of the wittiest and most perceptive reviews in daily journalism.

Glenna was assigned by her bright editor, Herman Kogan, a historian of note, to cover the Yukon doings. The Marshall Field syndicate would service her reports. She turned out to be the sole representative of the US press. Judy Crist, then editing the Sunday *Herald Tribune*, had contracted for her to do some exclusives from Dawson.

My favorite photographer, Eileen Darby, was in her native Portland, Oregon with her brood when I arranged for her to fly up to Dawson and cover the mad doings. She often covered Broadway productions for *Life Magazine*.

The Canadian Press was well represented. In fact, so en masse was their equipment that the DC3 Glenna and I flew from Whitehorse toward Dawson, had to turn back because it couldn't get high enough to clear the mountains. I was pleased with the decision the pilot made to return to Whitehorse when I looked at the wings and saw mountains higher than both spans. It seems that the American Broadcasting Corporation's dual language equipment and crews ( English and French) so weighed us down that we couldn't rise above the passes.

I pleaded with the ticket counter at Whitehorse that I had to be in Dawson City that night to supervise the dress rehearsal photo session with Darby, otherwise my whole trip had been in vain. They relented and put us back for the second try. This time we climbed comfortably over the mountains.

Whatever hour it was on the clock didn't much matter that far north in late June. It was daylight around the dial. My wife had thoughtfully packed a flashlight thinking I might need one. Once, at 3 AM, I got up, went to the bank of the Yukon River and photographed that mighty torrent and its anchored paddleboats by available natural light. No flash needed.

When I returned with the Darby photos of the event for the Sunday sections in The *New York Times*, Sy Peck was dismayed. The shot of the kiltie band from Whitehorse, which had tooted outside the Palace Grand at its inaugural, seemed to be in broad daylight. "Damn it, Sol," exploded the usually un-agitated, soft- speaking Peck. "I requested a night shot of the exterior, and look at this." I answered, "Sy, that is night up here. It was taken at 8:30 PM and, as a matter of fact, that's as dark as it ever gets on July 1 in Dawson City." "Oh, of course. Sorry."

Those zany, round-the-clock days and nights in Dawson stand out in my memory.

*Bert Lahr plays a perfect Foxy*
*with all the intended innuendoes*

I have flash-backs of Johnny Mercer up from Hollywood, out- drinking the bearded sourdoughs; dour Ring Lardner, Jr. and Ian Hunter praying Lahr could remember his lines, and urging Larry Blyden to feed them to him; Robin Craven, the epitome of Mayfair, with his darling bride, Babs, sitting in a huge bed of daisies, picking them for their cabin, oblivious to the world; Beatrice Lillie, aka Lady Peel, stepping from a helicopter as guest of honor of the Northern Affairs' welcoming committee, (Tom Patterson, chairman; Mrs. Bert Lahr and Mrs. Robert Whitehead) vastly enjoying the incongruity of the whole contrivance.

The cast rose to the occasion. Lahr was absolutely smashing in the title role and Blyden was a perfect foil. The romantic leads, Mary Ann Corrigan and Bill Hayes, were adorable.

The whole show was right for the time and place with Bobby Lewis, looking more than ever like a Tibetan Buddha, as he smiled happily at his charges. Dawson City was charmed.

But where were the audiences to come from? I had been so alarmed by the lack of advance sales that I resorted to lettering my own handbills on 8 X 10 copy paper and delivering them around town myself at the banks and bars. After opening, I consulted with Larry Elliott, the *Readers Digest* Canadian correspondent. He suggested I go with him to Anchorage, where he knew everyone because of his annual treks across the Dominion from his Long Island home. Maybe we could wrestle up some customers there. I readily consented.

I recall the editors of both Anchorage papers welcoming a visiting Broadway-ite with some amazement, and a Woman's Page editor telling me the definition of an Alaskan; "You have had to give up and go back to the lower 48 twice, then come back here for keeps a third time."

We did get some hard-core theatergoers to fly over and the local airlines were happy to publicize the event and to dig up some business for themselves. But Robin Stanford, Tom's assistant, said it all as we trudged around the Yukon hills that tourist-less summer, "We lack impulse buyers." We sure did.

I learned from Manager Gilkey that the hardest task was "papering" the house weekdays. However, thinking creatively, he enlisted native support. The Indians found it fun, and came night after night. They could easily have cued the cast if any forgot their lines, Gilkey thought.

Lahr found the fishing spectacular, and would trek via jeep and canoe into the outback to cast for graylings. He exhausted himself bouncing over corduroy trails. But since he didn't subscribe to the Stanislavski method and had no matinees, it didn't seem to affect his performance.

All of us returned south with prodigious hangovers from the Yukon hospitality, but vowing to return some day.

*Foxy,* co-produced by the Canadian Government, which was anxious to promote tourism in the area, ran for seven weeks in the summer of 1962. The producers ended up losing their $400,000 original investment. As for the Canadian Government, your guess is as good as mine.

*Foxy,* two years later, lived up to its Festival billing as "pre-Broadway," when it opened at the Ziegfeld Theater, again with Bert Lahr in the title role. On the night of its premiere, February 16,

1964, David Merrick is rumored to have sensed its doom.

Merrick unloaded his shares on the usually canny Billy Rose, proprietor of the Ziegfeld. Rose was so certain it was a hit, so the story goes, that he offered to purchase Merrick's share on the spot. Two hours later, when the notices hit the street, Rose had a splendid tax deduction, if nothing else. It ran for only 72 performances.

Although the publicity didn't fill the theater it made great copy. Arthur Gelb of the *New York Times* ran a whole article in its Sunday Section, including a map of how Bert Lahr and company got to the Yukon.

Gelb is not a common name, and yes, it is his son, Peter Gelb who is now General Manager of the Metropolitan Opera Co.

*A Silver Lining*

Henry J. Scott married Adele Hammerick of Philadelphia and fathered three daughters, the eldest of whom was Adele. Adele married Maurice Saul and they had two children, Robert and Barbara.

Robert was killed in WWII when his PT boat came under friendly fire from the Australians. As their PT boat began to take on water, Captain Robert Saul decided to swim to shore, believing that by reducing the weight in the boat there would be a better chance of his crew making it to shore. Even though Robert was an excellent swimmer, when the crew finally hit the shore line Robert was nowhere to be found. He left a wife and two small children.

When Barbara Saul was in her twenties, she married Harry Sprogell, a member of her father's law firm and they had four children, Prudence, Carolyn, Robert, and Jonathan.

While married to Adele Hammerick, Henry Scott had an affair with Jessalyn Brearley Richardson, from Minnesota, and this union produced Barbara Scott, who was called "Bobbie." When Bobbie was eight, Adele Scott passed away and Henry Scott married Bobbie's mother Jessalyn and adopted her daughter Janet Richardson, Bobbie's step-sister.

So, my first wife's father was Henry J. Scott and my second wife's grandfather was Henry J. Scott. I love telling people that my second wife was my first wife's niece as well as her godchild, and that Bobbie and Barbara were just a year apart in age.

While my wife and I were vacationing in Norway in 1968, Bobbie complained that she didn't feel very well and had pains in her lower abdomen. When we returned to the United States, at the suggestion of our family doctor who suspected Bobbie had more than just the common stomach ache, we sought help at the Lenox Hill Hospital in New York City. That was the hospital of choice for those that worked in the entertainment industry and was an excellent diagnostic hospital, especially for cancer illnesses.

It is difficult to put into words the feeling that one has when the attending physician says that your wife has uterine cancer. For the patient, it is impossible to imagine how devastating such a diagnosis is, with questions of "why me?" and "how long do I have?" and "is there any treatment to extend life?" For the loving husband whose wife is the focal point of his life, who must face the reality that his lover, his friend, his soul mate may well die, it becomes a nightmare.

Yes, the doctor said, there was a new treatment for uterine cancer; the use of cobalt pellets which could not cure the disease but well might put Bobbie in remission.

So, that's the path we chose; Bobbie underwent treatment for months and then recuperated with plenty of bed rest. When asked by friends how she was feeling she said, "I am fine, except I have cancer." Bobbie was an incredibly brave woman.

In retrospect, I should be grateful for the three years during which Bobbie was in remission, but in 1971, the dreaded disease returned to take over and, on April 4th of 1972, I lost my dear wife Bobbie.

On that day, my whole world collapsed. I just wanted to lie down and quit. My girls, Judy and Babs, couldn't have been more attentive and although they had just lost a mother whom they adored, there was no way that they could understand my loss.

They say that love doesn't die but that's little consolation to the widower. Death is so final. I wondered if I would ever be whole again. Thank God that I had my work to keep me busy.

Barbara Saul Sprogell was not only my wife's relative but one of my wife's devoted friends along with her half-sister Janet. They grew up together as girls, the Scott house and the Saul house being in close proximity to each other in Rose Valley, separated by a meadow. Although they were one year apart in school, they attended the same high school, and luxury transportation was supplied by the Saul's chauffeur, Arthur Rich.

*Back row from left: Barbara Saul, Janet Scott*
*In front of Janet, to her left: Bobbie Scott*

Arthur did more than drive the girls to school. He had been a star basketball player in high school and he taught them how to play the game "boys' style." He instructed them to pass the ball with force, hard and straight, rather then in a slow arching curve that allowed their opponents to constantly intercept the ball and score. As a result, the girls played on the varsity team at school and helped win many championships for the school.

Phebe Anna Thorne High School was an "open air school." In England, in the later part of the 19$^{th}$ century and the first part of the 20$^{th}$, the "open air school" was part of the English educational system. The idea of an outdoor school was based on the theory that fresh air and sunshine would do much to keep colds and other sicknesses away, especially tuberculosis. Even in winter the windows and doors were kept open and students had to dress warmly in heavy coats with hoods. The American "open air school" was located on the campus of Bryn Mawr College, Bryn Mawr, PA in what looked like three Japanese tea houses with sliding doors and windows that could easily be opened to the elements in order to let the fresh air inside. Pictures taken in the late 20's show students sitting at their desks in their tea house classroom with snow on the ground outside. Barbara insists she never got a cold or missed a day of school due to illness.

*Phebe Anna Thorne School*

Bobbie Scott left the Phebe Anna Thorne School at the end of her junior year to attend the Tower Hill School in Wilmington, Delaware. Following graduation, Bobbie enrolled in Bennington College which had just opened its doors; the year was 1932.

Barbara Saul no longer needed transportation by Arthur Rich; she could drive herself to school, now that she was 17, in her new convertible Ford.

Barbara Saul also left the "open air school," but she traveled overseas to Paris to study with Madame Nadia Boulanger. On returning home she was to attend Smith College, where her father had enrolled her prior to her trip abroad. However, Bobbie was so enthusiastic about her freshman year at Bennington that she convinced Barbara to join her at Bennington, rather than go to Smith. They ended up in the same dormitory in a four-room suite.

After college, the girls became even closer friends and, when the two women married, Bobbie Scott to me and Barbara Saul to Harry Sprogell, we two men also became good friends. As our kids started arriving, our two, Judy and Babs, and the four Sprogells, Pru, Lynn, Rob, and Jonathan, would get together occasionally either at the Sprogell farm in North Wales or at our house in New Hope.

Harry was a very successful lawyer at his father-in-law's firm of Saul, Ewing, Remick and Saul. As a Quaker in good standing at Gwynedd Meeting, he was one of the founders of Foulkeways, the Continuing Care Retirement Community (CCRC) where Barbara and I later took up residence in 2002.

One of the terrible jobs that I, as a widower had to consider was what to do with my late wife's clothes. Barbara Sprogell came to the rescue and offered her help. She was good enough to come to our New York apartment and help pack up Bobbie's clothes to be given to the American Friends Service Committee. As a thank you, I remember taking her to dinner on 57th Street and then up to Lincoln Center for a small concert at Alice Tully Hall. It was a memorable evening; we were two souls in mourning. Harry had died just a few months before Bobbie. We found we very much needed each other. And because both of us knew each other's partner, we could talk about the deceased easily. As the months passed we found we had much in common and, on January 1st, 1973, we were married in a Quaker wedding at Barbara's parents' house in Rose Valley.

We knew only too well that our marriage would be difficult for some of our children to accept. They had lost a mother or father and, from their point of view, our going together and eventual marriage looked to them as if we were trying to replace their parent. Well, I can tell you there is no way you can replace a deceased spouse. But what we both hoped to find was another loving relationship. And as for "replacing," Barbara Sprogell was quite different than Bobbie Jacobson and I was the antithesis of Harry Sprogell. Harry was much more formal; he had a wonderful sense of humor but would say it with a straight face whereas I would tell a joke with a smile and a wink. I was always thinking outside the box, while Harry thought like a lawyer.

From the loose tongues in the community we heard it all:

How could you consider marriage so soon after the death of your respective mates: don't you believe in an extended mourning period? Our answer was quite simple; the cancers of our spouses had gone on for years and our mourning had not started the day of death but rather when we learned of the seriousness of their respective illnesses.

After our marriage, Barbara left the North Wales farm and moved into my house in New Hope and to our New York apartment. Over the years, our relationship became even stronger and was verbalized often by, "Barbara, I love you," to which Barbara would answer, "Sol, I love thee, too."

*Scene* **9**

*Fiddler on the Roof*

*Zero Mostel as Tevye sitting on his milk cart*
*In "Fiddler on the Roof"*

There isn't a press agent alive who doesn't dream of that miracle run, the show that opens on Broadway like a bursting, glorious, sunny day and runs for years. It not only means steady employment and a constant meal ticket but it also takes some of the pressure and anxiety off the press agent as he wonders from where his next job might come.

*Fiddler on the Roof* was that kind of show. It ran on Broadway for eight years, along with out of town productions throughout the US and overseas, before it ran out of steam. And when it finally quit on Broadway, it was resurrected many times and is still one of the most popular musicals in America today. That says a lot about the universality of the show and, as we know, you don't have to be Jewish to connect with it.

And the royalties; those who were lucky enough to put their money in *Fiddler* from the start earned $ 1,574 for every dollar they invested.

I was one of the lucky ones. Carl Fisher, who was the money manager for his uncle, George Abbott, put together a small group of investors of which I was one. My share was $ 150. We pooled our money and invested in four shows; *Pajama Game, Damn Yankees, West Side Story* and *Fiddler on the Roof.* Not a bad group of shows as an investment. Can you believe, I am still getting checks on a yearly basis at the age of 97?

Sholem Aleichem, which translated means, "peace be with you," or "goodbye" or "hello", was the pen name of Solomon Rabinovich, a popular Ukrainian writer of the latter part of the 19th century who wrote about Eastern Jewish life in the "shtetl." He wrote about the trials and tribulations of "shtetl" life where Eastern European Jews were separated from the general population and confined into small villages because anti-Semitism was rampant, fueled by edicts from the Russian Government. He penned his stories in Yiddish rather than Russian or Hebrew, so the Yiddish speaking, semi-illiterate Eastern Jews could read his works. Many called him the "Mark Twain of Eastern Europe." He was a humorist, writing his stories without ridicule or flowery language. Shtetl life was hard but his stories said, "Laugh and be above it" and "Come, it's not as bad as you think; let me show you the brighter side."

American home libraries were filled with the complete works of Mark Twain; The Eastern Jews of Europe, filled their book shelves with the twenty-six works of Sholem Aleichem.

The story line of the musical, *Fiddler on the Roof,*' is an adaptation of the many Sholem Aleichem stories about "Tevye the Milkman." Perhaps the reader remembers the scene where the wealthy butcher, Lazar Wolf, wants to marry Tevye's eldest daughter, Tzeitel. Tevye agrees on such an arrangement only to learn that daughter Tzeitel will have none of it, for she is in love with the tailor Motel. Tevye relents but doesn't know how to tell his wife that the pending marriage is kaput. So Tevye cooks up this awful dream, awaking his wife in the middle of the night screaming that Lazar Wolf's late wife, Fruma-Sarah, has come back

*Tevye and Lazar Wolf agree that Lazar, the rich butcher, can marry Tevye's daughter, Tzeitel*

*Tevye cooks up the "dream scene"*

*In the dream, Grandma Tzeitel appears as a ghost and tells
Tevye that his daughter, Tzeitel, should marry Motel the
tailor and not Lazar Wolf*

*Tzeitel marries her true love, Motel*

271

as a ghost and is furious that the young Tzeitel would take her place as Lazar's wife, wearing her jewelry, etc. Another ghost appears that of his wife's grandmother, who states how thrilled she is that Tzeitel is going to marry that fine tailor Motel Kamzoil.

Tzeitel married her true love, but it marked the ending of the traditional relationship between the generations. The destiny of the Jews of Anatevka is bittersweet at best.

If you read the original "Tevye the Dairyman and the Railroad Stories" as translated by Hillel Halkin and look at the chapter headed "Today's Children," it is all there. Joseph Stein was the genius who was able to adapt this and other Sholem Aleichem stories into such a remarkable musical. Add the music of Jerry Bock, lyrics by Sheldon Harnick, the direction of Hal Prince, and the choreography of Jerome Robbins, and you've got a winner on your hands!

When Hal Prince and Ed Griffin set up the corporation to finance *Fiddler on the Roof,* the musical had no title. For convenience sake, and to put it on the books to raise capital, it was referred to as *Tevye.*

We were to open in Detroit at the Fisher Theater, a structure built by Fisher of Fisher Bodies and owned by Dave Nederlander, a mogul who owned a series of theaters throughout the country.

I had a problem; the musical didn't have a title and you can't sell a show without a title. I needed to print window cards and other advertising material.

Hal said Tevye sounded like the name of a Japanese typewriter.

Jerry Robbins came to the rescue. Jerry was a frequent visitor to art museums and art shows, collecting ideas for his dance routines by observing the various poses of the dancers portrayed on the artists' canvases. It happened that he was studying a Marc Chagall exhibit and one of the constant themes in Chagall's works is of fiddlers floating around, showing the "joy of living." One painting in particular that caught Jerry's eye was that of a fiddler with his foot on a roof top. That sparked the idea of calling the play, "Fiddler on the Roof." Jerry checked it with Hal, who liked the idea but who said, "Call Sol; see what he thinks."

I'll never forget the phone call. I was sitting in my office in the Selwyn Theater building on 42$^{nd}$ Street when Jerry called. "What do you think of the title 'Fiddler on the Roof'?" he asked. I didn't have to think, I was so excited. "It's wonderful!" I said. "I'll get our ad agency working on it right away." And they did, creating a caricature of Zero Mostel fiddling on the roof, using the Chagall motif. The image was also put into the text and the score to justify the appellation.

The new title solved my problem; I could now develop the advertising that I needed in Detroit. However, another complication arose: Detroit's three papers were on strike. Fortunately, all was not lost; the editors, friends of mine, still wrote reviews and they gave them to me to use. The *Windsor Star*, in the neighboring town of Windsor, Canada, printed my story and we were able to print window cards and handbills. Dave Nederlander had a creative idea: if I would make up heralds or handbills, he would hire a group of kids to place them under the windshield wipers of the cars that were parked in the synagogues' parking lots around town. He did, and the crowds came to our opening.

On one of the nights during our Detroit stay, Blue Cross/ Blue Shield bought the house out as a fund raiser. Just as soon as the curtain went up, the audience told us it was going to be a booming success; they flipped out!

Timing has a lot to do with the success of a show. Some shows are born lucky, others not. Remember *The Admiral's Daughter* with Jose Ferrer, a comedy set in Hawaii about romancing by a sailor? It opened on December 6th, 1941. It didn't have a second night; the attack on Pearl Harbor took care of that. *Fiddler* was born lucky.

After a successful tryout week in Detroit we moved the show to Washington and, thanks to our concentrated efforts to publicize the show, all went well and the crowds appeared. That week also gave the director time to cut, trim, polish and rewrite. That's really why the tryout cities are so important to fledgling musicals before they open in the Big Apple.

*Fiddler on the Roof* made its New York debut on September 22, 1964, at the Imperial Theater. It ran for 3,242 performances, achieving the longest run for any musical up to that time.

To celebrate opening night, we had a party at Roseland on 57th Street for the cast and the backers. We all knew we had a winning combination and the notices agreed. Even Brooks Atkinson wrote a rave review. The songs were clever and melodic, the kind an audience could readily hum once they left the theater.

The day after we opened in New York there were lines of people stretching from Broadway to 7th and then to 8th Avenues, two city blocks long. All were cued-up waiting to buy tickets. If that doesn't indicate that the show is going to make it big, nothing will. And the lines didn't subside. Theatergoers even stood in the rain to obtain tickets. One rainy day I had some umbrellas silk-screened with the *Fiddler* logo and gave them out to those wet ticket seekers who were in line. Photos were taken and sent to the media. If nothing else, it was a hell of a publicity stunt; we got great coverage by the media. It made very good press.

We started sending out national press releases reporting what a hit *Fiddler* was and the advance sales grew so large it was difficult to print tickets fast enough. Many times there was standing room only. I had never witnessed anything like it in all my years on Broadway.

A few days after we opened on Broadway, I received a call from my former employer and friend, Dick Maney. "Sol," he said, "Congratulations; *Fiddler on the Roof* is going to outrun them all. You are even going to outrun my show, *My Fair Lady.*" He was right on; we did.

Soon after the opening, Hal sat Lou and me down in order to review our tactics. Realizing that *Fiddler* was not only going to be a hit but would run for a long time, Hal decided, and wisely so, that the emphasis in promoting the show should play down the ethnic nature of the very Jewish Sholom Aleichem story to make it universal. The ad for Jewish rye bread that showed a Native American chewing on a piece of rye bread, with the headline, "You don't have to be Jewish to enjoy Jewish rye bread" is a good example of achieving universal appeal.

Hal didn't tell us how to achieve universality; that was up to us. Happily, we started to have overseas productions which were enthusiastically accepted by many different cultures such as the Japanese and the Germans. When the Soviets started attacking Jewish dissidents, just as the Czars had done before them and as portrayed in *Fiddler*, our musical became even more plausible to our audiences.

When Hal Prince realized that Zero Mostel was going to be with the musical less than a year, we had to think about shifting *Fiddler's* advertising and publicity campaign. Zero's contract read, "From the first day of rehearsal, one year." And he was adamant; one year and that was it. His real love was painting. He wanted to be an artist, not an actor. When I asked him what he really wanted to do, he told me, jokingly, "I want to play King Lear because it typifies a nice Jewish family." Oh well, I never did understand actors and Zero, although a funny, fat and lovable human being, was extremely difficult to work with from a publicist's point of view. Zero lived above a flower shop on 23$^{rd}$ Street with no telephone. The only way to contact him was through the flower shop, asking the florist to ask him to call us. And as for getting Zero to interviews to promote the play, forget it: Zero would say, "Hell no, Sol, you've got a hit on your hands, the theater is full, and you don't need me." Why did he act that way? God only knows; I realized years ago, actors are a talented but strange bunch.

Zero committed some outrageous behavior on the stage playing Fiddler. He tended to get bored with the role rather quickly and would invent new stuff to keep himself interested. He committed excesses on the stage because they were funny. Everything Zero did was funny but not necessarily right. For instance, in one of the performances, Tevye's hand "accidentally" fell into a pail of milk, and for the next three minutes the play revolved around him wringing milk out of his sleeve. It was more of a distraction than funny and added nothing to the content of the play.

Not only did Zero have a contract for only a year but he insisted he take a vacation during the third month, for a month. So the caricature of Mostel as The Fiddler in the ads and logo gave way to the motif of the more Chagall-like little fiddler, as devised by Jerry Robbins on stage, the symbol of happiness who shows up to mime and fiddle whenever Tevye, the milkman, is feeling good. That the press agents gave Luther Adler, Zero's replacement, a rare publicity barrage when he took over for the month while Zero went to Europe to gaze at the Prado in Spain and the Klees in Berne was unique.

Would the show, only three months old, survive Mostel's absence? Mr. Prince found out quickly that *Fiddler* didn't depend on just Mr. Mostel; it was a show that could make it on its own. Not that every Tevye here or abroad didn't incorporate some of Mostel in their characterization. But Zero was generous with Luther Adler, working with him on stage before performances, helping him with nuances and quick changes, all the technical things he had acquired in the months of rehearsals and tryouts.

When *Fiddler* was just as joyously received in such outposts as West and East Germany, Israel, Holland, France, Britain, and Japan, we had plenty of publicity ammunition. The most difficult problem was finding out when the overseas versions were being unveiled and then alerting the network of internationally minded newspapers and wire services. Best results were obtained in Germany when an Israeli actor speaking German played Tevye to acclaim. The Germans were among the most enthusiastic *Fiddler* fans. We played to sell out crowds every night. It was difficult for me to understand why the Germans accepted *Fiddler* with its obvious Jewish content. You go figure.

In Tokyo, a Japanese film star wowed them. Especially touching to Japanese audiences were the incidents of breaking with tradition by Tevye's daughters, marrying without consent and out of their faith, "How could it be anything but a Japanese problem? So like us," they exclaimed.

When the Japanese asked whether *Fiddler* had been a success in the United States and were given an affirmative answer, they retorted by saying, "Strange, but it is so Japanese"

In South Africa, we had a particular problem. Apartheid was the law of the land and Americans didn't want *Fiddler* to be presented in a country that was under boycott from the United States. However, the South African producer came up with a brilliant idea: would the Americans send *Fiddler* to South Africa if the producer shared some of the profits with the South African Black Theater? It worked. Fiddler would be done and I was there, as press agent, to help in its success, writing feature stories and visiting editors of local newspapers. The fact that the Black Theater Community was sharing in the profits was newsworthy. All in all, it was a wonderful production and well received by the South Africans.

Creativity is the backbone of a good publicist, and every once in a while we flacks have to think outside the box. Keeping in line with Hal Prince's insistence that *Fiddler* had to have a universal appeal, my thoughts turned to," What can we do now that *Fiddler* has outrun *Hello Dolly*?" To celebrate the occasion, I felt that music would attract attention; but what kind? The logical choice, a Klezmer band, was too parochial. But a band was needed, so I went to the New York Police Department and hired their Scottish band in full uniform, kilts and all. Soon they were playing in front of the theater that marked the occasion and the resulting publicity was smashing.

*Fiddler* would be my swan song with Hal Prince. As press agent, *Fiddler on the Roof* was by far my longest engagement; I ran with it for nine years until it ran out of steam in the middle 1960s. Hal asked me to be his exclusive press agent but I turned him down as I had with so many others who wanted exclusivity. I liked the idea of being able to pick and choose multiple shows; an agent with associates could run as many as six different shows at one time. I liked running my own business and creating my own schedule; I still enjoyed those summers off with my family.

Hal needed an exclusive press agent and Mary Bryant fit his bill. Mary no longer worked for me as an associate and had set up her own Press Agency. She gave that up and became Hal's full time flack.

*Fiddler on the Roof* was one of the most successful shows ever to hit the Broadway stage and in 2010 is still thrilling audiences throughout the country. A friend of mine, Theodore Bikel, at the age of 86 recently played Tevye to a sellout crowd in Tucson, AZ, taking Chaim Topol's place because of Chaim's sore shoulder. Theo was well prepared to fill in. He has played Tevye more than two thousand times, more than any other actor and he received a standing ovation from the audience. He attributes his ability to play the milkman to the fact that his grandfather lived in Eastern Europe in a shtetl and was "poor as dirt." Theo feels that when he plays the part of Tevye, he is really playing the part of his grandfather.

*Fiddler* ranks alongside *Sound of Music* as a favorite with parochial schools, even today.

My working days started to slow down after *Fiddler* although I did work as a flack on 22 more plays into the early 1980s. My last Broadway play was the comedy, *Horowitz and Mrs. Washington.*

The call from Barney Frank was a real surprise. At that time Barney was a member of the Boston Massachusetts Town Council, a State Representative and an assistant to the Boston Mayor.

He wanted to run for the U.S. Congress and asked if I'd be his manager. I thought it was a pretty funny request and, with a laugh, I said to him "What the hell do I know about Boston politics!" But I did give him an idea that helped him get elected. I told him to get a New England newspaperman who covered the State House to start writing articles about him and about why he should be in the U.S. House of Representatives. It must have worked because Barney is still in Congress, representing the Massachusetts 4$^{th}$ district and, as of 2010, is chairman of the all-important Financial Services Committee.

# ACT IV

★ ★ ★

## Enjoying Retirement

# Long Lake, New York

If you draw a large circle in the northeastern part of the state of New York making the area the size of the state of Vermont, you will have created the Adirondack Park. The park was established in 1882 and given state constitutional protection so that part of the area would be protected forever. Forty percent of the land is controlled by the State Forest Preserve Commission, while the rest is owned privately. The park became a National Historic Landmark in 1963.

It was smack in the middle of Adirondack Park that Maurice and his brother, Walter Saul, wanting to escape the hot summers of Philadelphia and be where the air was pure, disease free and the water clean, looked for a summer home. In 1927 Walter found his Shangri La, not too far from the small village of Long Lake. Not to be outdone by brother

Walter, Maurice started looking in earnest in 1928, a year before the Great Depression.

On a summer day in the latter part of the 1920's, Maurice was schmoozing with Ann Plumley and enjoying a piece of her famous pie. Ann ran a camp for guides on Long Lake and, during the conversation, Maurice spoke of his wish to buy a place on the lake and of his inability to find something that fit his fancy.

"Oh," remarked Ann, "there is a place for sale eight miles up the lake. In fact, Doc Jennings, who has been caretaker for the property, told me the other day that the owner would like to sell."

"Where can I find Doc Jennings," Maurice asked?

"He happens to be sitting right over there," she told him.

A quick introduction to Doc, a trip by boat - there are no roads - to see the sixty-acre property, and the deal was consummated, with the proviso that Doc Jennings stay on as caretaker.

My wife, Barbara, was thirteen and her brother, Bob, a few years older when the summer home on Long Lake was purchased. The property did come with some buildings; a main house, a cottage for the caretaker, and a boat house.

Because of the property's isolation, Maurice knew he would need proper water transportation to get back and forth to the town of Long Lake. He called his friend and insurance agent, Charley Seltzer, instructing him to go over to the New York Boat Show and purchase the following; a Chris-

Craft for himself, a motorboat for son Bob and a 17-foot Luder's Red Wing sailboat for Barbara. Charley was tickled to oblige.

Barbara Saul spent most of her summer teen years at Long Lake and continued summering there after marrying Harry Sprogell. Children and then grandchildren enjoyed the fresh air and the clear water of the Adirondacks. For Barbara, Long Lake was her escape from the big city and she loved it. They called their private camp "Boulder Beaver."

I had trouble adjusting to this "idyllic" spot on the lake. It was too calm for me; there was little for me to do. I was a city boy and liked the excitement of knowing what was going on in the world, so having a radio at my disposal as well as the daily papers, especially the New York Times, was very important. At first, neither of these was available until I did manage to hook up a short-wave radio with the aerial attached to the copper plumbing at the kitchen sink, but the static made it difficult to hear. Nixon's "Farewell Address" in August of 1974 was only slightly audible. In later years I did get delivery of the New York Times when the local mail boat delivered supplies to our camp. Needless to say, my prized paper was rarely current.

As for swimming in the lake, it was too cold, but I worked out a pseudo solution. I began my swimming experience by boiling water in a tea kettle on the wood stove. Then, carrying the kettle down to the lake, I entered the water. Once in, I turned around slowly, releasing the hot water all around me. At least it took the chill off. After many years I did resolve that problem by purchasing a hot tub which Barbara's son, Rob Sprogell, cleverly heated with propane. Barbara and I enjoyed a dunk every night with an occasional view of the glorious Northern Lights.

I loved to read at night but that was a problem for we had no electricity until the early 90's. We did attempt to read by kerosene lamp, but that had its own innate problems. The light was not bright and put a strain on the eyes, but worse than that, if the lamp was not watched carefully, the Kerosene would run dry causing a flame-out which coated the lamp's glass chimney with ugly black soot. Being the absent-minded professor that I am, this was a frequent occurrence with me. However, ingenuity being the mother of invention, we worked out what we thought was a pretty good system to give us more daylight. We set all our time pieces two hours ahead which meant "real time" might be 7:00 PM while our "camp time" was 9:00 PM. This meant that when we retired at night it was still daylight and we could read, It all worked out quite well except that once in a while we forgot we were on "camp time" and arrived at another camp for invited drinks and hors d'oeuvres two hours early.

It wasn't until twenty-five years later that electricity was installed, thanks to a series of solar panels and a huge bank of batteries. Our family finally realized that reading at night was important to Barbara and me.

In order to give me a little more insight as to what I did and did not do at "Boulder Beaver," I asked my Grandchildren to give me their thoughts with the proviso that I wouldn't edit them. I keep telling myself that only those that love you can make fun of you and get away with it:

## Grandson Stephen Magee:

During the summer I would spend several weeks or more with my Grandparents, in the woods at "Boulder Beaver." It became one of my favorite places on earth not only because of the woods and the water, but it meant time I could spend with my Grandparents.

My Grandfather had many charms and skills but directions, reading a map, and driving were not in his quiver of skills. He was famous for his "shortcuts" and everyone in the family was subjected to them. Invariably we would end up lost and the trip might take double the time that it should have. But there was a positive side; we did get to see many parts of the country we had never dreamed of seeing and meeting some interesting people when we found them to ask directions.

When it came to driving, Grandfather, whom we referred to as Morfar (Grandfather in Norwegian), had a heavy foot. One day he was stopped for speeding. He claimed the speedometer was broken so he didn't know he was over the speed limit. The officer was not impressed. Neither that explanation nor his silver tongue could wangle his way out of the ticket. With his accumulated points he was required to go to driving school to keep his license where he found himself the oldest member of the class by at least 30 years. One of the youngsters asked him "Hey, Grandpa, what-cha you in for?" He was always able to tell a good story and, to this day in family lore, he blames it on the faulty gauge in the car.

It was a real treat to have ice cream at camp. Morfar used to like to make it with our help. An avid berry collector of both blueberries and raspberries, he always had gathered enough to flavor the heavy cream. We began by using our old wooden ice cream maker. We'd dump the ingredients in the stainless steel canister, placing the paddles, called a dasher, into the mixture, cap it with the stainless steel lid and settle it into the outer wooden bucket. We packed the bucket with ice and rock salt, hooked up the handle on the top and started cranking out ice cream. We grandchildren would take a turn or two but, as the cream solidified, cranking got harder to do and the grownups would take over. When the dasher refused to turn, we knew the ice cream was done and we would be enjoying our freshly made ice cream. Making ice cream with Grandfather was one of the highlights of the summer along with that first taste, for we, as the grandchildren, were allowed to spoon the fresh ice cream off the dasher as it emerged from the ice-cream maker.

An incident happened when I was nine that I remember as though it was yesterday. Morfar and I were canoeing on the lake, he in the stern and I in the bow. As we paralleled Pine Point, the camp where my cousins lived, Grandfather's wrist rubbed against the canoe's gunnels, opening the clasp on his prized gold watch. We both looked in horror as the watch slipped into the cool water and spiraled to the bottom of the lake. Now my Grandfather had always been the cool, collected gentleman around his Grandchildren so I was amazed at the swear words that burst forth from his mouth.

I, unlike my Grandfather had a very good sense of direction, and was able to quickly fix our position by lining up three positions. Once back in camp my Grandfather told the sad tale of his watch loss.

You can imagine my surprise when my grandmother was able to contact a scuba diver in Long Lake who was working on one of the docks that needed repair. He agreed to dive for the lost watch. Within the hour he arrived with his gear and the three of us started out towards Pine Point. I was allowed to go along for I had never seen a scuba diver before and to me it all looked like magic.

By the time we got to the spot that Grandfather was convinced would yield his watch, the light was beginning to fade as evening approached. A number of dives came up with the same result; no watch. The Scuba-man reported only seeing dead rotting leaves on the mucky bottom. Finally, I'd had enough and with a great deal of courage, I tugged on my Grandfather's shirt to get his attention. In a small voice I squeaked that we were in the wrong location and I knew where the watch was. I had the correct position if they would only listen to this nine-year old.

Begrudgingly they moved the boat some 100 feet to my position but warned only two more dives were possible; the sun was setting and Mr. Scuba Diver was running low on oxygen. Nothing was produced on the first dive, but the next, and our last, revealed the valuable watch.

Morfar was ecstatic. The watch had been found, and I was the hero of the day. My grandfather was happy to have his watch back and I was happy to be on his lap as we drove the boat back to camp. It was one of the best sunsets of my life.

## Granddaughter Gaelen VanDenbergh:

My sister Jennifer and I used to spend many summers at Long Lake with Sol and Barbara, at Boulder Beaver. Some memories I have of Sol: He loved to be in charge of certain kitchen duties. He also insisted upon preparing the hors d'oeuvres for the many cocktail parties that they hosted. These were also pretty terrible - he liked to prepare mussels from the lake (they are best used for fish bait), on stale Ritz crackers, with cheese and ketchup, that he would heat in the oven. We all ate them! I eschewed the mussels, I confess.

Sol or Barbara always read a psalm at breakfast, in their bathrobes, in the sun-filled kitchen.

Yes, the psalms which Sol edited (!) - in pencil only - to adapt the references to the flora and fauna to where ever they were at the time, either PA (lilacs, frogs peeping), or Long Lake (bunch berries, loons calling), or Key West (bougainvillea, roosters crowing). He crossed out all the references to "smiting" anybody, and made the references to "man" and "mankind" gender neutral, although, references to God remained "He".

## Granddaughter Jennifer VanDenbergh:

He always made us terrible (unbeknownst to him, of course) blueberry pancakes, made with blueberries that he would pick from the bushes in camp. I don't know why they were terrible. The recipe seemed sound enough. But Jen and I dutifully ate them while others made their excuses. He, he!

He claimed the recipe was from the Lowell Inn, in MA. He even had a business card from there with the recipe on it. But, when you are 8 miles down the lake with no road to take you there, in the middle of the Adirondack wilderness, you don't usually have all the right ingredients on hand. I doubt he was ever able to adhere exactly to the original recipe. And he was also cooking on a wood stove so it was impossible to control the temperature. Those pancakes were always burnt (Grandma said she liked them that way) on the outside and raw on the inside. And he cranked out dozens of them for the numerous grandchildren and guests.

Other than sitting to read a psalm, my recollection of Sol at breakfast was that he was always bustling around- tuning the radio, stoking the fire, pouring the coffee, cooking, opening windows, serving food. He was a morning person, and he liked morning chores because they kept him busy. I was fascinated by the fact that neither he nor Barbara ever dressed for breakfast. They got up very punctually at 8 am, but always in their night clothes and bathrobes. Sol did all his chores and ate his breakfast, had coffee, chatted on the porch, and then would retire around 10 am to get dressed for the day.

About those blueberries - they were fresh-picked, wild mountain blueberries. They are about 1/4 the size of a good garden pea, like small tapioca beads. They grow sparsely, about ten ripe to a bush. The bushes are low, no more than a foot square. Picking them was excessively time-consuming. If the entire household decided to dedicate itself to the task for an entire morning, we could pick enough for two small pies. It was one of Sol's favorite activities! It was a tedious task, outside in the sunshine, suitable for all ages and abilities, and he could talk the whole while, telling us stories of his career as a press agent for the theater, everything he knew and loved about New York, current events, worldly wisdom. It certainly passed the time, but as kids, we HATED it! We would so rather have been drowning in the lake, or wandering off into the woods and getting lost, or making trouble of any and every kind. And we certainly didn't want a several hour lecture about culture and art or politics. Having said all that, I will have to admit, as a mother of small children, I now look upon that experience as better childcare than any amount of money can buy!

I don't want to remember about the mussels. We're lucky we still have our livers and kidneys intact. I think collecting them was another tedious, time-consuming task which Sol used to fill up his days in the wilds. They made excellent fish bait. And over the years, the grandchildren were quietly encouraged by concerned adults, to raid Sol's mussel cache, a large, wire basket he kept in the water, tied to end of the dock. We were urged to use the captive mussels for fish bait so that they would NOT end up as hors d'oeuvres.

It took three years but Sol finally got the picture and freshwater mussels remained in the lake.

Sol was an avid birder. He loved birding in the Adirondacks, and why not you say, since he was well away from civilization and in the woods, summer after summer after summer. And it was NOT an activity in which the grandchildren were generally included because young children could NOT be counted upon to keep quiet or be entrusted with such expensive and wondrous equipment as binoculars, even though they were ancient and extremely heavy and I suspect army surplus. Also, the binoculars lacked the flexibility to be positioned to accommodate a narrow set of a child's eyes. I distinctly remember having to squint through one eye piece because the minimum width setting was too wide for me to see through both eye pieces at the same time. Incidentally, those binoculars are STILL at camp. Although these days, we use them to look at the boats passing by: "Oh look, is that the Pine's boat? Are they in camp this week?"

But Sol loved birding. It was an adult only activity, away from the grandchildren-riddled camp where everything revolved around preparing and cleaning up after 3 meals a day for an average of 15 or more people.

My father and his best friend were avid birders too, the kind who keep lifetime lists of the birds they saw. Yet avid birders made consistent excuses to avoid birding with Sol. However, my father resigned himself, with loud complaints, to birding with Sol twice a summer, a great sacrifice. This was because Sol did not, in fact, care what birds he saw. He was not even particularly knowledgeable about the native bird populations even after years and years in the Adirondacks. Birding was, for Sol, an outdoor exercise combined with child-free, adult (preferably male) conversation about the arts, culture or current events. In short, he wanted to TALK, uninterrupted by women obsessed over the lack of certain vital ingredients for whatever recipe, or the challenges of cooking on a woodstove, or the quaintness of the non-electric kitchen tools. If you really wanted to look at birds, you did NOT want to go birding with Sol.

Sol was interested in people; he was not interested in birds.

## Granddaughter Robin Magee:

I know the lack of transportation in Long Lake made my grandfather stir-crazy. He couldn't scoot out for a quick errand, chat with people & return. I know his need to get out and about fueled his enthusiasm for learning to "drive" the boats (badly) and definitely inspired his endless projects: berry picking, mussel hunting, checking on the spring, hosting cocktails, going out to other camps for cocktails, typing his thoughts about the theater and the people he had met, birding, and reading the latest "page turner."

As Jennifer & Gaylen remember it, the era of the mussel as edible was quite terrible. Morfar figured the only way that the mussels would taste OK was if he deep fried them and then dipped them in ketchup. In other words he had to get rid of any possible taste, but they were still barely edible.

Another tradition Morfar had was reading a morning psalm out of the Bible. At Boulder Beaver it was the Dartmouth Bible. He always read Psalm 121, which he called The Traveling Psalm, before we left camp or were headed out on a journey. I do have to amend the story of lighting at camp. Camp Time (putting the clock 2 hours ahead) was instituted by Barbara's father, Maurice, a practice they maintained until Rob Sprogell installed gas lighting throughout the main cabin in the late 70s. The gas lights enabled EVERYONE to stay up late reading books: Adele (Barbara's mother), Barbara, Sol & all the guests. After that it seemed silly to have the camp on a different time from the rest of the world (it did get in the way of socializing).

Some years we had a camp variety show in late July or early August. One year Rob did the most hilarious impression of Sol! He tied up a bandana Morfar style (knots on all four corners) the most important preparation for berry picking. His impression included impatience about the mail, the whereabouts of THE paper, making clippings from the obits section, and finding the perfect place for radio reception. Morfar loved it.

Morfar had all sorts of theories about how to get the best radio reception. Sometimes it involved throwing wires into the branches of overhanging hemlock trees (a specific side of the house, too). I remember getting hustled out of the kitchen during the Watergate Hearings because the absolute best reception was from the copper pipes under the dishwasher.

Morfar was always interested in everyone. He'd fold you into his project & then tell you about past adventures, crazy moments, people, scientists, theatre folk. Sometimes I was too impatient to listen and other times I absorbed the stories. After Henri & I were married, I remember Morfar spending time with Henri by getting him involved in the radio reception project of the summer at Boulder Beaver. One time when we visited them in Key West, Morfar had Henri come out for a walk with him to the grocery store/barista "The Five Brothers". Henri came back completely over-caffeinated from the "boccis" (powerful mini Cuban espressos) he'd been treated to. They also returned triumphant with that days' *New York Times.*

When I was about 13 my grandfather gave me a script of *The Barretts of Wimpole Street* for my birthday with an obscure note about how he'd worked with Katherine Cornell on this play. At that point in my life, I loved reading scripts (musicals, plays, my uncle's movie scripts) and I loved this one. It was only years later that I found out this was the play that saved my grandfather's life. He actually used that phrase "that is the play that saved my life" and he told me the story about being in France during WWII, seeing Katharine Cornell, and meeting up with an old friend, Lew Azarel who got him transferred to the 29th Division Newspaper for the duration of the war.

My grandfather was definitely short on patience with most members of his family. You needed to understand or do something right away and when you didn't he was quick to anger. I think he had lots of patience for his friends and professionals in the theatre business. I know he was good friends with many actors, artists and luminaries of that era as was my grandmother Bobbie. I remember hearing the story of a young actor, Earl Hyman, who was feeling very lost and my grandmother, would go for long walks with him and chat about what was going on with him. Earl became quite an important African-American actor in New York. He fell in love with the country of Norway, learned Norwegian and became a respected artist in Norway. He also became a foremost interpreter of Ibsen. I often wonder if my grandparents had anything to do with his Norwegian connection as they too loved Norway (& often visited).

My entire family lived in my grandparents' New Hope house for a year. My Aunt Babs and Uncle Paul would come out for long weekends or parts of the week from NYC (where they had an apartment). I didn't realize it at the time but my grandmother Bobbie was quite ill with cancer & I think my parents & grandparents thought it was a good arrangement to have everyone close by. Now when I look at the house I'm amazed to think that 9 people lived there for a year. It was in the country so we did have quite a bit of running around space. I remember my grandparents often had cocktail parties into the late hours of the evening. I used to sneak down & watch all the glamorous people or lie in bed wondering how they could make that much noise just having boring grown-up conversations! At least my brother & I could stay up late talking those nights because the grownups couldn't hear us over their noise!

My grandfather was working on *Fiddler* at the time. I loved that cast album and played it frequently. MorFar would storm into the living room growling, "Turn that blasted record off!". At some point he bought headphones so that the children could listen to their records without disturbing the adults. MorFar was an audiophile & had a great-reel-to-reel tape deck. He'd often interview Quakers, actors, and people he thought were interesting & record the interviews on his reel-to-reel tapes and later on cassette tapes (he loved the portability of them). Morfar always had a radio near his bed; when he couldn't sleep at night he'd listen to ball games & radio shows from various parts of the country. In the late 70's he said to me, "I've heard this funny show from Minnesota with jokes about Norwegian bachelor farmers and powdermilk biscuits. I think it will catch on." He sure was right about that. "The Prairie Home Companion" is still going strong in 2011! He was quick to catch on to new trends in entertainment. When I was 6 he said to me "Robin, there's a new show on TV out of New York with a talking frog.

I think you'll like it! It's on right now." Right then and there I watched my first episode of "Sesame Street."

I also remember that my grandfather had NO patience for commercials on television or radio. I think they drove him nuts! When we were watching TV (in the 1960s & 70s) he would get up, walk across the room and shut off the TV whenever a commercial appeared. He had an amazing internal clock because he knew exactly the right moment to turn the television or radio back on. This habit always had me in agony because I didn't want to miss a bit of what we were watching. Later, he loved the technology of the remote control! From across the room he could mute or turn off the TV!

Morfar has always had "itchy feet" or the need to travel and have adventures. Living between four different houses with Barbara completely suited his temperament. He loved knowing the best place for local foods, wines & entertainment. He truly enjoyed scouting errands. I remember him asking Barbara what ingredients she would like for that day's lunch or dinner & then he'd head out to procure fish from the fishmonger in Lambertville, green beans from a Bucks County Farm, and wine from the liquor store in downtown Lambertville, and something else from downtown New Hope. Some days he paced his errands out over the course of a day, stopping back in to deliver an ingredient and news of where ever he had been.

For all the complaints and idiosyncrasies attributed to me by my exaggerating grandchildren, when it came to summers in the Adirondacks, I did enjoy being there, in part because I could anticipate spending the winter at my favorite place, 618 Grinnell Street, Key West, Florida.

Now, I said that I would not edit the grandchildren's recall but, just to keep the record straight, the thick buttermilk sweet and sour pancakes come from the Lowell Inn in Stillwater, Minnesota, not Massachusetts. I found the recipe in one of the magazines I had been perusing. And, other than my grandchildren, I received rave notices from those who were fortunate enough to have a taste of my pancakes. My other specialties were the banana bread (I always used rotten, brown bananas) and pot roast in cider. I thoroughly enjoyed cooking.

Birding I did a lot of and kept a life list. Enough said!

*Foulkeways, my home:*
*A Continuing Care Retirement Community*
*(CCRC)*

Most of us don't like to think about growing older, becoming frailer and ultimately needing help with the tasks of daily living that we currently take for granted: But, truth be told, if we live long enough, few of us get to skip this final chapter of our lives.

The concept of a Continuing Care Retirement Community grew out of a need for an institution that would care for the aged during their last stages of life. It had to blend several components; a community that would include independent living, assisted living and skilled nursing care facilities. Best described, it had to be a step-down community where an individual has the opportunity of living independently in an apartment or a house but then, if needed, move into a more assisted environment.

The CCRC model is not a new concept but one that was conceived more than a century ago in Europe. However, one has to remember that the need for such an institution was not paramount in 1900, for average longevity was only 49 years.

In the 1960s, as Americans began to live longer, (in 2003 life expectancy was 77.5 years), the concept of continuing care took hold in the United States, beginning on the West Coast. Foulke- ways, founded in 1967 by Quakers, was the first CCRC in Pennsylvania and one of the first east of the Mississippi.

But it wasn't until the 1970s that the CCRC came into its own and by 2009 the American Association of Homes and Services for the Aged reported the existence of 1900 such facilities. The majorities of these are not-for-profit and have a faith-based affiliation.

Barbara and I decided many years ago that should we have need of a CCRC, Foulkeways at Gwynedd, PA would be our choice. Barbara, especially, had a vested interest. Both she and her late husband, Harry Sprogell, were on the Organizing Committee of the Gwynedd Friends Meeting when Foulkeways was conceived, and they played an active part in fulfilling its destiny.

Foulkeways might never have been built had it not been for Charles Beaumont's wife, May Foulke Beaumont, who on her death bed, had made a specific request of her husband; "When you die, leave our property to the Gwynedd Friends Meeting."

In 1945, the now widower Charles Beaumont had a premonition that he was soon going to die and, before he did so, he wished to make good on his late wife's request. So, he called Thomas A. Foulke, a well known local lawyer and a member of the Gwynedd Meeting, who lived in the area and was kin to May Foulke Beaumont.

It was a gloomy and stormy night but Thomas Foulke, curious as to what was on Charles Beaumont's mind, agreed to come to the large home with impressive pillars that stood on DeKalb Pike across the road from Gwynedd Meeting. The two men had never met.

Thomas A. Foulke was stunned when Charles Beaumont asked that his will be written, leaving his entire property to the Gwynedd Friends Meeting. But Thomas obliged and, on Charles Beaumont's death forty days later, The Gwynedd Friends Meeting became the owner of the Beaumont House, full of valuable antiques, and also two barns, the "Lowry House" and 67 areas of woodland and meadow. (It was fortunate for the Meeting that Charles did not die within 30 days of signing, for according to Pennsylvania law, the will would have been null and void.)

The property, dating back to the late 1600s, was part of a site established as the settlement to William Penn in a new grant from King Charles II of England. May Foulke's grandfather, Dr. Antrim Foulke, a member of Gwynedd Friends Meeting, had purchased the property in 1863. It was because of May's love for her grandfather and his devotion to the Society of Friends that she wished that the property be willed to the Meeting. She herself was a member of the Episcopal Church of the Messiah, just a short distance down DeKalb Pike from the Meeting House. Although she had been brought up in the Gwynedd Friends Meeting as a Quaker, upon marrying Charles Beaumont, a member of the Church of Messiah, it is assumed that she was "read out of the Friends Meeting," a custom in those days for someone who married out of the faith.

We Quakers are past masters of discussion, dialogue and creative thought. A committee to look into the possible use of the Beaumont property was established. In the ensuing years, a Friends' school was proposed that involved Germantown Friends School and Germantown Academy. Also proposed was an Intentional Community or commune for Quakers, an integrated community socially, religiously and economically. Many more suggestions were made and disregarded. Quakers believe reaching decisions by consensus.

Gwynedd Meeting member Edward Zimmerman had an idea. The year was 1958, 13 years after the Meeting had acquired the Beaumont property. Why not use the land as a retirement community for the aging, a "cottage type" facility which would include assisted living and long term care? He had watched the strain on his mother who had, in her kindness, taken on the care of his two grandfathers for many years during their terminal illnesses.

Another committee was formed, the Project Committee, to proceed with a feasibility study. Harry Sprogell was Clerk, with my wife Barbara, serving along with him. In order to learn more about continuing life-care communities Harry journeyed to California to inspect two facilities, the Carmel Manor in Carmel, and Sequoias in Portola Valley, California.

Then in 1963 William Clarke, a member of Harry Sprogell's committee, on his return from visiting a cousin living in a life-care retirement home in CA, reported enthusiastically about the pros of such a community. In the meeting of the Project Committee in April of 1963, the feasibility of building a continuing life-care community on the Beaumont property was again discussed and began to get some traction. After a few questions and answers, William Clarke, stood up and said, "Of course it can be done and we will do it."

In January of 1967 Harry Sprogell (I am sure with the help of my wife Barbara) authored *The Treasure and the Dream,* a copy of which hangs prominently in the main entrance of Foulkeways.

*The Treasure and the Dream*

*A message from*
*Gwynedd Monthly Meeting of Friends*
*To the Residents at Foulkeways*
*January 1967*

*Foulkeways at Gwynedd carries out a dream of Gwynedd Friends Meeting which began when a neighbor, (not a Friend) left a beautiful farm to the Meeting for use as a memorial to his wife May Foulke Beaumont. After much consideration the Meeting concluded that such a memorial could be created best if the farm were used to accommodate a community planned for older citizens where every feature of the architecture and the services could be designed especially for their needs, where facilities could be provided to meet every health hazard without disrupting family and friendly ties, where activities could be made available with their special interests in mind, but most of all where people could find persons of common interest and comparable age with whom to share the mature friendship and mutual support that only the rich experience of a lifetime make possible.*

*To the future residents of Foulkeways
Gwynedd Meeting gives with love
Its Treasure and its Dream.*

In true Quaker spirit, it took another 4 years, but on April 16, 1966 ground was broken, and the first residents of Foulkeways moved in during the Spring of 1967, more than twenty years after the property had been inherited.

When Foulkeways' idea was being developed, it needed capital and Harry Sprogell was asked to obtain a bank loan. As the story is told, the bank he approached was hesitant in lending money for such a progressive idea as a CCRC but, finally, relented. The banker said, "Harry, let's talk about the three Cs; Credit, Cash and Character. You have no credit, you have no cash, but you do have a great deal of character. On that we will lend you the money."

In 1991, Barbara and I sold our house in New Hope and moved back to Rose Valley, PA into Barbara's old home, the Saul Mansion, with Prudence (known as Pru), Barbara's eldest daughter, and her husband Larry Plummer. The Plummers had purchased the house in the 80's and were willing to have us Jacobsons as tenants. Our sanctuary was Barbara's old bedroom, a spacious room on the second floor; but, of course, we had use of the entire house.

During the ten years of our stay in Rose Valley, I was active with my old friends at The Hedgerow Theater and with the Friends Meeting in Swarthmore. Although there were two local Friends Meetings in the town of Media, we felt more comfortable at the Swarthmore Meeting even though the distance was greater.

My biggest problem living at the Rose Valley house was Pru and bananas. When in the Rose Valley residence I took up cooking and banana bread (James Beard's recipe) was one of my specialties. One of the ingredients was bananas that had ripened and were brown. I carefully put these out in the pantry only to find them missing when I needed to make my bread. Pru invariably, thinking that my bananas were rotten, would discard them. Many a day I had to retrieve my perfectly ripened bananas from the compost.

In the latter part of 2001, Barbara and I decided that now was the time to move into Foulkeways. I was going to be 90 and Barbara, 88. What the future would bring we could not foresee but we knew that the time was right to be in an environment that would take care of us if need be. I knew the transition would be easier for Barbara for she would be returning to her roots and the many friends she had had at both the Gwynedd Meeting and at Foulkeways.

Early in the spring of 2002, Nancy Gold, of Admissions, called us to say an apartment, a one bedroom expanded unit, was ready for us if we wanted it. In June we moved in.

Entrance economics were simple enough. A large payment was made to secure our apartment, which is non-returnable should one remain in Foulkeways for more than five years. A monthly charge for the apartment allows the resident full use of all the facilities and activities offered. There are no extra charges for services.

I always viewed this upfront money as an insurance policy against the possibility of needing a more assisted living environment such as Foulkeways' skilled care facility. In my brief study of what happens to an elderly person's finances if they require nursing home care, I concluded that health care was not only expensive but could easily drain one's financial resources with alacrity.

Our move went smoothly, and although I was concerned that I could no longer be as independent as I used to be, this seemed trivial in terms of the whole picture. And I found a new set of friends who could enjoy my stories of Broadway. Boredom was not a problem either, for Foulkeways offered choices from a hundred committees! I zeroed in on Current Events and would come to the meetings with clippings of articles in hand, ready to discuss them with others. The Library and Movie Committees were also among my favorites.

Judy and Babs, my two daughters, and the Sprogell children were pleased with our move but, as loving and helpful as they are, they just don't get this "old age business." They call this the Generation Gap and it is so true. Our kids have their own problems and are at a different stage in life. Theirs are ones of employment, bringing up kids and filling their days with their various activities. A required nap in the afternoon is an enigma and not even considered.

All of us realize that this is the last stop in our lives and that death, although we wish it to be many years from now, is inevitable. My kids hate this statement but it still says it all, "There is no alumnae association at Foulkeways."

Ongoing construction at Foulkeways has been monumental beginning previous to our entrance into the community. Gwynedd House, a state-of-the-art, skilled nursing care facility was completed in 2001. It continues to receive national accolades. It truly is unique; built like the spokes of a wheel, each room looks out onto greenery. Rooms are single but there is enough space for another bed if need be. Carts in the hallways are non-existent. All patients' drugs are locked in their individual rooms giving the hallways a non-cluttered look. At the hub of the spoke is a dining room with seating capacity for 16, next to a small kitchen where the food is prepared. Each floor has four spokes.

The old Abington House, our assisted living quarters for members who needed assistance but not full nursing care, was updated and modernized into suites. These attractive apartments provide a large bedroom plus a living room and small kitchen.

Following 2002, the greatest rebuilding of Foulkeways since its inception began thanks to the foresight and vision of the Foulkeways Board and Foulkeways' executive director, Doug Tweddale. Living in the 21st century required some creative thinking if we were going to compete with other new CCRCs that were emerging in the area.

The small, single apartment was no longer king; those applying wanted more space. Combining two one-bedroom apartments and making them into two-bedroom apartments or one- bedroom with den solved the problem. The call for something even larger fostered a new type of building; 26 town houses in a new section named "Tyson."

After seven long years of backhoes, gravel, cement, plywood, fiber board, metal struts, insulation, stucco and paint, plus the expenditure of some 36 million dollars, a new Meadow Café, an enlarged and completely renovated dining room, an auditorium with the latest in sound, light and stage and seating over 250 people, and a small food store which supplied some needed essentials for daily living plus a lot of goodies for the palette, completed our project.

Recognition of our wonders caught the eyes of Medicare who awarded us their highest five star rating, while *US News and World Report* listed Foulkeways as one of the 100 best skilled nursing care facilities in the country.

But the award of which we are most proud is the 2010 *Pathways to Greatness Award* given by Larson Allen, LLP. CPAs, Consultants and Advisors to AAHSA (American Association of homes and Services for the Aging), which recognized Foulkeways as the best aging service organization in the nation. How were we selected? Here is how:

"Pathways to Greatness recipients are selected by a panel of industry experts who evaluate five key attributes of a successful aging –services organization: leadership, superior performance, distinctive impact, best practices and innovation, and the ability to inspire public trust and confidence." (footnote #)

The facilities are without question, simple elegance. Some now call Foulkeways "The Four Seasons at Gwynedd." And how many residents can go out of their apartments, exercise by walking their campus for 45 minutes following trails through thick woods with a stream and still be within the confines of their own property of over one hundred acres? In Spring, when the crocuses and daffodils are in bloom, a walk becomes an extra treat. For those who wish a more structured program, our exercise gym and pool, staffed by professionals, satisfy their needs.

But, beautiful modern surroundings and a large campus don't tell the story of why, almost to a person, we express the same cliché when we get up in the morning; "Thank the good Lord we live at Foulkeways." It is our fellow travelers and the employees at Foulkeways that make the difference. All of us together are the "Spirit" of Foulkeways.

Understanding each other at this stage of life is one of the great pluses of living here. We have like souls to talk to, commiserate with, and enjoy. They understand what that hip replacement was like, that hospital trip for dizziness, or all those pills we ingest. And all this understanding and interest in others is what builds friendship and community. At Foulkeways we become an amorphous group, a large family who are genuinely interested in each other and each other's well being. Eating meals together in our main dining facilities or coffee shop further solidifies this community.

Basic Quaker values are woven into the fabric of Foulkeways, which accepts all members whether staff or residents as individuals living and working together to the same end. This no doubt is why we have such a small turnover in staff, an industry low of 6%.

All this adds up to a unique, caring community. Barbara and I are so glad we are here.

★          ★          ★          ★

In 1938 I joined our union, ATPAM, the Association of Theatrical Press Agents and Managers. By 2009 I was the oldest living member of the union.

My joining the union was hardly voluntary. It became a requirement for my continued employment with the Shuberts. My employer at the time, Claude Greneker, came into my office one day and said, "You better join the union if you want to work here because the Shuberts just signed a contract and it stated that they would not hire anyone who did not belong to the union."

Before the birth of our union, press agents were fair game. For example, a producer might hire an agent to open a show in Chicago. The press agent would hustle to Chicago a few weeks before the opening to make the proper arrangements, only to find that if the play was a flop, the producer wouldn't pay up. The hard working agent was left holding the bag.

All that changed with the birth of ATPAM, thanks to the hard work of Roy Henderson, Helene Deutch, and Dick Maney who fostered the idea of a union to protect their fellow press agents. They described the job of a press agent as:

"An executive who handles one or more legitimate attractions for producing managers and is responsible for the publicizing and exploitation of such attractions."

Following the formation of the union, if the agent was hired for a particular show, a written contract was drawn up guaranteeing his or her salary. There were strict regulations regarding press agents and their associates as to how many shows could be handled at one time. If an agent was running two plays he was required to hire one associate. Four plays, two associates, six plays, which was the limit, three associates. Associates' salaries were set at $150 to $175 per week.

In June of 2009, arrangements were made for some of the old press agents and photographers to meet in the union headquarters in New York City and talk about the days of yore.

Much to the consternation of my family and friends, I hopped on the train at Gwynedd, PA which delivered me to center city Philadelphia, where I transferred to the bus that took me to New York. From Penn Station in New York City it's not a long walk to the union headquarters on W 45th street.

As Ralph Blumenthal of the New York Times put it, "The one-liners zing as veterans of flackdom remember legendary exploits."

And so we did. Flack Bob Ullman, who at one time worked for me, reminded us of this anecdote:

In the 1962 play *Here Today,* Tallulah Bankhead was supposed to pick up a ringing phone onstage and set the action in motion with her conversation. "She forgot her lines," remembered Ullman, and she handed the phone to her surprised co-star, saying, "It's for you."

Shirley Herz, who worked with Bob Ullman in a partnership, recalled working for another press agent, the legendary Samuel J. Friedman, when women were just getting started in the field. (This was the same Sam Friedman who took me under his wing when I worked with Claude Greneker). Sam complained that by having women in the office he could no longer curse his usual blue streak.

I reminded the group of my run-in with David Merrick when he had a stooge in the audience run up on stage and slap one of the actors in the show *Look Back in Anger*. At first I was taken in by the action but, when I learned the story was a hoax, I went to my friend Bill Glover, the A.P. critic and let him know the real story, which he published.

It was old home week. Leo Friedman, the famous photographer, age 90, flew in from Las Vegas. If you wanted studio shots, Joe Ables, Leo's partner, was the one you called. For scene shots, it was Leo. Perhaps the most famous shot was that of Carol Lawrence pulling her lead, Larry Kert, through the slums of New York.

(Actually, Leo told me, the scene was shot in Manhattan in a very nice section and in order to make it look like a slum, trash cans were introduced.) The pavement was marked with a chalk line and as the two actors ran towards the camera, that was where Carol was supposed to look up as Leo took the shot. Carol reported that it took 300 shots to get the right one and she was worn out.

*Carol Lawrence pulling Larry Kert on the streets of New York West Side Story*

We ended the delightful get-together with a question: with the changes in the business over the ages, did young people still dream of becoming press agents?

The answer, "This is not the group to ask".

★         ★         ★         ★

In 2010, another example of my stubborn desire to travel independently happened early on Monday morning, November 9th following a conversation with my friend, David.

Sol: "David, I can't meet with you this AM at 9:30; I have my semi-annual meeting at the U of P with my cardiologist, Dr Irving M. Herling."

David: "Ok, but how are you getting to the hospital?"

Sol: I have arranged for a driver to take me to the Gwynedd station; I'll hop on the train and then take the bus to the hospital. Did you know there is a wonderful loop bus that takes you right to the hospital?

David: "Sol, what time do you want me to pick you up? I'm taking you down."

Sol: "You don't have to do that, there really is no need. It's all arranged, I can----------------"

Now for the record – I don't think there is anything worse than two old, stubborn, German Jews arguing about what they can and can't do. Independence is wonderful but there are times when the younger of the two has to take a stand.

David: "Sol," (his voice dropped and lost its sweetness.) "What time shall I be in front of your apartment complex? 11:30?"
Two more repeats of "David, I hate to make you do that," and 11:30 was the settled time.

The trip into town was uneventful and the traffic was doable. We got to the hospital well ahead of the scheduled 1:20 appointment. Parking in the Penn Towers Garage, we walked over the bridge, down hill, into the main hospital only to find that Dr. Herling's office was now in the Penn Towers Building. So, it was back over the bridge and, unfortunately, uphill. I was having trouble breathing and my mobility was slowing. We stopped so I could catch my breath. What I neglected to tell David was that I was having chest pains and I had been popping Nitroglycerin pills to ease my angina.

We finally arrived at the Doctor's office and, fortunately, with a little urging from David, the staff realized that I should be seen immediately.

Half an hour later, after seeing Dr Herling, I reappeared in the waiting room.

Sol: "David, they want me to check into the hospital."

David: "OK, what did the Doctor say?"

Sol: "He said I have two choices. I could leave now and plan for my funeral because I was about to have a serious heart attack or I could check myself into the hospital."

We spent time in a holding room waiting for a bed in CICU and, at one point, David called Dr. Herling's assistant, Roz, to see if she could hurry things up. She referred to him as "the driver" which tickled him immensely, never having had that appellation before. Roz's magic must have worked; by three o'clock I was safely in my single hospital room in the Founders section of the main hospital, with the medical staff doing their thing.

A catheterization was performed the next day and more drugs were prescribed. My saying the "Sh'ma" must have worked for I was to be discharged by 11:00 on Wednesday and I felt 100% better. I talked with David and he asked me how I was getting back to Foulkeways. Same litany, "I am going to take the bus, train, etc."

David insisted on picking me up. We even stopped at the Water Works restaurant for lunch, my treat.

Everyone was much relieved and pleased to see me on campus sitting in my apartment in my favorite chair.

Because of a sore throat and feeling of weakness, Barbara and I cancelled our Florida trip, but only for a few days.

On Sunday November 22, 2009 we left for Key West.

*Scene* **3**

# *Key West, Florida*

Key West, Fl is the most southern city in the United States. It is 160 miles from Miami and 90 miles from Cuba.

The city was hit hard by the Depression; 85 % of the local population was on welfare. So bad was the situation that the authorities suggested the island be vacated and the inhabitants resettled in Tampa, Florida.

It was the Governor and the New Deal administrators who saved the day. They concluded that the best hope for Key West was to make it a haven for tourists. They began by inviting artists from all over the country to Key West to paint murals, design monuments, produce plays, and write books, with the hope of enticing vacationers to their city. It must have worked because, in the years that have followed, Key West has become an enchanting vacation spot and famous writers like Ernest

Hemmingway and Tennessee Williams are residents.

Under the auspices of The WPA (Works Progress Administration), President Franklin D. Roosevelt appointed F. Townsend Morgan, a Philadelphia entrepreneur-turned-artist, Director the of the Key West group of artists. In the middle thirties, Townsend, with his family, moved to Key West.

In 1936 Townsend, a good friend of the Sauls (my second wife's family) invited Adele Saul to the Island for a visit. "Perhaps you'd be interested in buying some real estate here," he suggested. And, "Why not bring your daughter, Barbara, with you to keep my daughter, Mary, company?" Barbara and Mary were childhood friends both growing up in Rose Valley, their houses separated by a driveway. As Barbara put it, "Mary is my best friend."

Adele fell in love with the island and although her husband, Maurice, was in London at the time, she convinced him that real estate on Key West would be a good investment. It took some doing; for the first two properties in which Adele had an interest, sold before she could get her husband to agree on the purchase.

Adele finally took matters into her own hands and, without her husband's consent, bought the house at 618 Grinnell Street paying the down payment of $100 with her own funds. Later, Adele purchased the house next door which granddaughter, Lynn, and Grandson, Rob, currently occupy. Daughter Pru purchased just a block-and-a-half away.

In Barbara's words, "In 1936 it was a most enchanting place to be. It reminded me of Paris when I was a student of Madame Nadia Boulanger. Hemingway was here and so were a lot of other artists. During the day they work hard and at night we'd party. I remember dancing on the tile floor of the Havana Madrid Club on Front Street and at the Bird Cage Club at the Casa Marina. It was quite an experience for a young lady of twenty one."

Even before marrying Barbara I knew of the existence of the white clapboard house on Grinnell Street for I had visited Adele with my first wife, Bobbie. Previous to Bobbie's death, Adele had asked us to visit her in Florida feeling that the salt air and sunshine would be helpful to my wife's deteriorating condition.

Early settlers to the island had had difficulty finding materials to build their homes. However, the conch shell was abundant. By burning the conch shell and extracting its lime, the settlers made a mortar of sand, water and lime that was used in the construction of their homes. Thus the name "conch house" was coined. Even when wood was introduced, the name stuck. But construction became quite different with more thought given to the movement of air, especially during the hot Key West summers.

The wooden "conch houses" were built on pilings to allow air to circulate under the house which prevented the foundation from rotting. The interior rooms had high ceilings and a high pitched roof that offered space for dormers and, thus, more circulation of air. Large windows and ceiling fans also helped.

The Saul's "conch house" was built in the late nineteen hundreds and was typical of the architecture of the surrounding houses. During the subsequent years, the kitchen was expanded to add a pantry and roofed porches on both sides of the house that were accessible from both the kitchen and the pantry. The outhouse and the outside pump were replaced with a bathroom for the two rooms on the second floor. A bathroom was constructed on the first floor attached to the master bedroom and another bath with shower was built behind the kitchen. The upstairs facilities were without a bath or shower because to quote Adele, "I don't want my guests to be too comfortable or feel too much at home. If they need to shower, let them use the first floor bathroom." Just to make sure that her guests would not be "too comfortable," a shower head was included that had not been changed in years so that the water trickled from the fixture.

As for modernization of their conch house in the years that followed, forget it. Adele liked it the way it was and, after Adele's death, we felt the same way and made no changes other than the usual repairs like a new roof or an interior coat of white paint. It remained a 1930 retro, with its original windows and doors, a kitchen and pantry of wood with linoleum on the floor and shelving to hold our Flemington pottery. No modern fancy cabinets or

Dupont "Corian" countertops. There was one exception, however; a microwave to heat leftovers.

After my marriage to Barbara in 1973, this is where we would spend our winter months. It was a place I thoroughly enjoyed.

When in Key West, I always liked to read the *New York Times* in the morning but found that there were no deliveries of the *Times* to stores within walking distance. So, I called the circulation department in Miami and a nice young lady asked if she could help. "Yes," I said. "I am an old drinking friend of Max Ginsburg who was Circulation Manager of *The New York Times*. We used to have drinks at Sardis after work. Could you tell your manager to leave some papers off at the Five Brothers in Key West? It's an easy stroll from our house."

And that's how the Cuban Deli known as The Five Brothers, began carrying the *New York Times*.

One of the projects I enjoyed and which kept me out of trouble while in Key West was my connection with the Literacy Volunteers of America of Monroe County. Since 1984, this institution has helped over 4, 000 students achieve personal goals through increased literacy skills. I have been a member of this organization since its inception and have had the pleasure of dealing with students from all over the world who want to learn English. Their classroom is my living room on Grinnell Street or our porch, if it's not raining. In 2007 I was honored at a luncheon and was told that I was their oldest living volunteer. I guess I was at the age of 95.

For years the movie theaters of the area did not supply what I felt the public needed; films that had better content and were equal to the intellect of their viewers. Art and foreign films fit into that category. When I first started my campaign for better movies, I visited with the manager of one of our local cinemas. I asked, why couldn't he bring us better films? His blunt retort, "We're in the popcorn business, not the film business. That's how we make our money and better pictures won't sell popcorn!"

And this is why in 1998, an old carpet depot warehouse on Eaton Street, in the heart of Key West's Old Town, was converted into the Tropic Cinema Theater, showing first rate films of all kinds. Through the work of many hardworking and devoted people in the community, our building now houses four theaters. We are a nonprofit and according to Mimi McDonald, a Board Member, we raise more money than any other non-profit organization in Key West. And the biggest plus of all? It is in walking distance for most people in town.

Another one of our theatrical interests was in the Red Barn which was built in 1829 and used originally as a carriage house. Through the backing of many interested people who gave of their time and money, the Red Barn is now a first rate live theater, considered one of the three professional theaters in the State of Florida. Barbara and I were honored when they named the Atrium after us.

Although we had a car at our disposal to haul our heavier needs from the store, our bicycles were our main means of transportation. It was easy to do because there are no hills in Key West; it is flat as a pancake. I was amazed that in my early nineties I was still riding, "Isn't it wonderful that I can still ride this two-wheeler and not kill myself." The library, were I worked as a volunteer and where Barbara was president, was an easy ride as were many of the other institutions that we used.

For entertainment we frequented the Red Barn and the Tropic Cinema Theater but on special occasions we would be entertained by Bobby Nesbitt on his magical piano when he performed at various spots around Key West. Bobby was trained as a classical pianist but preferred the rhythms of Gershwin, Berlin and Rodgers more than Beethoven and Brahms. He not only played and sang the show tunes but would give backgrounds and histories of the songs and their composers. Bobby and I were buddies and I enjoyed filling him in on some stories that he didn't know. He always saved us the best seats in the house.

We served juice and cookies and, once a month, there was a pot luck lunch. That was part of the agenda for Sunday morning services at the Jacobson's house with as many as 25 people in attendance. If the weather was inclement, worshipers took their seats in our large living room. In the Quaker fashion, all sat in silence until someone was moved to speak. If we were lucky enough to have a nice day, our side garden, filled with blooming bougainvilleas, orchids and an array of other Key West flora was our sanctuary. Quaker meeting meant a great deal to me. No rabbi, priest, or minister to officiate; congregants were on their own to create the kind of religious experience that was meaningful to each. And following my harrowing infantry experience in WW II, I became an avid pacifist, protesting war of any kind.

*Barbara and Me in our Key West home, January 2010*

As Barbara and I reached our early 90's we found that house- keeping chores at our Grinnell home became more and more difficult. Simple chores such as shopping, laundry and cooking meals were no longer simple. Fortunately, Barbara's daughter Lynn, living next door, took over the running of our household. Evening meals were prepared by a couple in the neighborhood who delighted us with delectable dinners. Whenever anything needed fixing Rob, who lived in the same house with his sister in an upstairs apartment, made it work again. Pru, living down the street, watched over the whole operation. Judy, my daughter came to visit, from Ann Arbor and I would speak regularly to daughter Babs, who lived in the New Hope area. Jonathan Sprogell, Barbara's son helped with our finances, keeping our books in order.

What I am trying to say is that our children pitched in to take care of the "old folks", for which both Barbara and I are eternally grateful. In our favorite Key West they allowed us to live a full life.

*Scene* **4**

## *Words of Love and Life*

The trip to the hospital and the near death experience gave me an opportunity to pause and reflect on my 97 years on this earth. My doctor had told me in no uncertain terms that my arteries were clogged and there really wasn't much that could be done. Old age had finally caught up with me. Physically, I was in pretty good shape, able to ambulate, although a little slower and I did have a slight stoop when I was upright. As for the head, it was working fine. My most immediate concern was for my wife. I had bluntly told family and friends that "her mind was shot." This was true but difficult for me to accept. Alzheimer's was affecting Barbara's daily living and I was worried about what would happen if I were no longer around to take care of her. Our social service department at Foulkeways gave me peace of mind. Foulkeways was equipped to handle such contingencies with an assisted living unit and a section for the Alzheimer patient. I made the decision that once we came back from our winter in Key West we would both go into the assisted living unit, giving up our cherished apartment. But back to those reflections:

I feel I've led a charmed life. Every step of my progression into the theater seems fortuitous. It started by my sneaking under the curtains to see Eddie Cantor in Atlantic City, then came Hedgerow and the Erlanger, followed by New Hope Playhouse, my summer in New Hampshire, and my becoming part of the New York flack scene under the tutelage of C. P. Greneker and the Shuberts, Phyllis Pearlman and George Abbott, and ending before the war with the King of Press Agents, Richard Sylvester Maney. After being discharged I created my own shop with a succession of successful shows such as *West Side Story* and *Fiddler on the Roof,* a total of some 200 plays/musicals in all.

The theater meant the world to me. Not only did I enjoy my work as a press agent but it allowed me an entrance into the world that few have. As a press agent, actors, managers and producers were dependent on me to publicize their shows, making sure the public knew their production was in town and they the public, should see it. And I got to know these theater people on an individual basis which I thoroughly enjoyed.

The theater represented something else to me. I knew the ending. Whether it was a play, a musical, or whatever, it always had the same ending. I knew that Maria and Tony would die in the last act of

*West Side Story.* I was sure that the abolition of the town of Anatevka would disperse the Jews of Russia in *Fiddler on the Roof.* The theater was a make-believe world in which I always knew the ending. This was a far cry from real life where conjecture is omnipresent when one thinks about the future. The theater allowed me to retreat into another world. To me it was magical.

Couple the above with a life full of love on the home front and indeed I feel charmed.

In my memory I hear Walter Huston singing Kurt Weill's haunting "September Song" to Maxwell Anderson's lyrics from the Broadway show *Knickerbocker Holiday.*

I see my centenarian mother-in-law, Adele, waltzing and singing to herself as a chanteuse had chanted the song in a Key West club.

Now I sing it to myself, a nonagenarian dreaming on our patio in Key West, Florida while the sun kisses the exotic flowers in our garden. Like all good poems, it speaks to my condition.

Have I learned anything over all these decades?

Maybe.

But What?

To know how fortunate I've been to love and be loved.

To listen to others in love.

To know the only thing I'm able to change is myself!

★          ★          ★          ★

Sol Jacobson died on February 17$^{th}$, 2010, in the 97$^{th}$ year of his life, quietly slipping away in the hospital in his beloved Key West, with family attending him.

Perhaps the best epitaph that we can give Sol Jacobson is one that his wife Bobbie inscribed on a set of Sean O'Casey's books; "To Sol, the dearest, sweetest man I know."

## ★ Acknowledgements: ★

First and foremost to my loving wife, Patty Ann, who edited the manuscript so skillfully during the writing process. This was a necessity and a tremendous help to this dyslexic.

Judy Magee and Babs Zimmerman, Sol's delightful daughters and my new-found friends, encouraged my writing about their Father and even said, "You have brought him back to life," a compliment that I take to heart.

Jimmy Hirschfeld, three-time Emmy winner, for his work as producer/director of Captain Kangaroo, has been a close friend since we were five. His encouragement and input into this work have been invaluable.

Arnold Trueblood, an Earlham College classmate and successful Businessman/Builder, is a bloodhound when it comes to finding spelling errors and misplaced commas. His careful combing of the manuscript has been a tremend-ous help to me and to the reader.

Peter Bauland, Professor of English at the University of Michigan and a cousin, helped structure Sol's story with specific emphasis on authenticity of the material.

Thanks to Ken Hiebert, Professor Emeritus, The University of the Arts in Philadelphia, for his very professional help in cleaning up some of the old pictures so they could be printed.

Alex Teslik, Eileen Darby's grandson and curator of Eileen's massive collection of photos of Broadway shows and performers, has given Sol's book an added dimension by tying the text with Eileen's remarkable pictures of the past. Thanks is hardly a strong enough word to express my appreciation to Alex.

Carolyn Sprogel, Sol's step-daughter and keeper of the Key West house, was most helpful in saving all of Sol's notes and papers that he had stashed in the attic of the Grinell Street House.

Thanks to the various Grandchildren who sent me fond memories of their Grandfather's idiosyncrasies.

Thanks to Actress Blythe Danner who was kind enough to read the manuscript before its printing and to write such beautiful words, not only about the book but about her times in the Jacobson household.

Thanks to Hal Prince, Producer/Director who has garnered 21 Tony Awards, who wrote such a meaningful introduction and who shared his knowledge of the theater with my PAL and me in his office at Rockefeller Center.

Thanks to Elizabeth Meade Howard who was kind enough to share her writings about Sol and Barbara with me.

And thanks to the many readers who read the raw manuscript and caught various mistakes and typographical errors: Tuck Brennen, Dick Stiller, Dick Robertson, Marianne Kalman, Sally Nangeroni, Jeanne Brenman, Dr. Gus Beck, Dr. Frank Clark, and Shirley Herz.

Thanks to Nancy Nolan, Director of Marketing and PR at Foulkeways whose enthusiasm and professionalism were great motivators.

Thanks to Ron Stone, a student at Gwynedd Mercy College, who recorded his interview with Sol and made the DVD available to me.

And last, but not at all least, is Barbara Saul Sprogell Jacobson who believed in what I was doing, who listened with pleasure to my readings and who loved Sol and gave him great happiness.

If I have failed to mention the name of others, please know you are appreciated and chalk it up to my advanced age.

## ★ Credits: ★

Sol's many personal interviews with me, augmented by written material from his files.

Wickipedia – Used as a powerful source of information and an excellent way to check dates.

Hank Whittemore's Memoir – *Word Press.com* Hank was good enough to let me use a direct quote from his memoir.

Cardcow.com – Order Number: 14325 Postcard Scan of Forty Niners Chase Barn Playhouse, Whitefield, NH

Al Hirschfeld's: The Bucks County Play House ©AL HIRSCHFELD. Reproduced by arrangement with Hirschfeld's exclusive representative, the MARGO FEIDEN GALLERIES LTD., NEW YORK.WWW.AL HIRSCHFELD.COM

Al Hirschfeld's: *The Tea House of the August Moon* ©AL HIRSCHFELD. Reproduced by arrangement with Hirschfeld's exclusive representative, the MARGO FEIDEN GALLERIES LTD., NEW YORK.WWW.AL HIRSCHFELD.COM

Billy Rose Theatre Division, The New York Public Library for performing Arts: Friedman/Abeles: 2 Photos from West Side Story

1) Carol Lawrence pulling Larry Kert down the
street Licensing Agreement No 44149
2) Stephen Sondheim, Arthur Laurants, Hal Prince,
Robbert Griffith, Leonard Bernstein, and Jerome
Robbins on stage
Licensing Agreement No 44142

Eileen Darby Images Inc. Alex Teslik, Eileen
Darby's Grandson is in charge of the Darby
collection of photographs at:
www.EileenDarby.com

Jason R. Long – Recent graduate of the Ringling
College of Art and Design who designed and
created the Book Cover.

Photo of the Author by renowned Philadelphia
dentist, Dr. James Dannenberg

# ★Bibliography★

Morigi,Gilda, *The Difference Began at the Footlights: A Story of Bucks County Playhouse* (The Collegian Press, Stockton, NJ, 1973)

Michner, James A., et al, *The Genius Belt: The Story of the Arts in Bucks County, Pennsylvania* (Pennsylvania State University Press, 1996)

Bikel, Theodore, *Theo: The Autobiography of Theodore Bikel,* (Harpercollins, 1994)

Zimmerman, Blanche, *Foulkeways: The Treasure and the Dream,* (Celo Valley Books, Burnsville, NC, 1992)

Shaeffer, Louis, *The Reminiscences of Sol Jacobson,* Oral History Research Office, Columbia University, NY, 1976

Aleichem, Sholem, *Tevye the Dairyman and the Railroad Stories,* (Shocken Books, 1987)